# IT TAKES ENDURANCE

# IT TAKES ENDURANCE

### EUGENE ROBINSON

Multnomah Publishers *Sisters, Oregon*

IT TAKES ENDURANCE
published by Multnomah Publishers, Inc.

© 1998 by Eugene Robinson

International Standard Book Number: 1-57673-454-4
Printed in the United States of America

Cover photo by Jimmy Cribb
Used by permission of the National Football League

Scripture quotations are from:
*The Holy Bible,* New International Version
© 1973, 1984 by International Bible Society,
used by permission of Zondervan Publishing House

Also quoted:
*The Holy Bible,* King James Version (KJV)
*New American Standard Bible* (NASB)
© 1960, 1977 by The Lockman Foundation

*Multnomah* is a trademark of Multnomah Publishers, Inc.
and is registered in the U.S. Patent and Trademark Office.
The colophon is a trademark of Multnomah Publishers, Inc.

For information:
MULTNOMAH PUBLISHERS, INC.
POST OFFICE BOX 1720
SISTERS, OREGON 97759

Library of Congress Cataloging-in-Publication Data
Robinson, Eugene.
    It takes endurance / Eugene Robinson.
        p. cm.          ISBN 1–57673–454–4 (alk. paper)
    1. Robinson, Eugene. 2. Christian biography—United States. 3. Football
players—United States—Biography. I. Title.
BR1725.R6245A3    1998                                    98-36325
277.3'0825'092—dc21                                       CIP
[B]

98 99 00 01 02 03 04 05 — 10 9 8 7 6 5 4 3 2 1

# TABLE OF CONTENTS

# ACKNOWLEDGMENTS

First, I would like to thank the Lord Jesus Christ for saving me June 10, 1984, and creating a new person.

I would also like to acknowledge my wife, Gia, for demonstrating unconditional love, and my children, Brittany and Brandon, for allowing me to be Dad.

Last, but not least, I want to thank my pastors, Ken Hutcherson and Carl Payne, who have been extremely instrumental in my walk with the Lord.

# PREFACE

There's a trend in our society today, and I think it's a dangerous and unhealthy one. We live in a day and age where endurance isn't a high priority in people's lives. We want what we want, and we don't want to wait for it or work hard for it. We want results, and we want them now. When the going gets tough, too often we want to bail out rather than see something through to completion.

I believe it's like that in the Christian world, too. Too many of us, when things get tough—as the Bible promised us would happen when we attempt to live a godly life—we shrink away in frustration or fear when we should be looking to God for our strength and motivation.

I believe there's a better way to live, and that is to place your faith in the Lord Jesus Christ, who, through his Holy Spirit, will give you the strength to endure whatever tests and trials come your way. To me, that's the definition of success!

Living the Christian life isn't easy. That's because it goes contrary to everything this evil, fallen world stands for. As Christians, we are called to live a holy life that is wholly and completely dependent on God. The world, on the other hand, says that we should do what we want and should look to ourselves to provide for our needs.

That way has been tried for ages, and it just doesn't work. In the end, the way of the world brings only dissatisfaction and emptiness. It is only those who rely on the power of God who are able to endure, to ultimately succeed.

Jesus put it bluntly when he talked about accomplishing anything for the kingdom of God: "Apart from me, you can do nothing." The key to endurance is relying fully on the power of God. Ultimately, you are telling God, "I can't do anything without you."

I have written this book first to encourage you to commit your life to Jesus Christ, then to offer encouragement so that you can endure the testing of your faith. I want you to realize that if you rely on God, there's nothing you can't do. I want you to look at my life as an example of what someone can accomplish if they put their faith in God and allow him to lead the way.

I'm nothing special. Yes, I've played on two Super Bowl teams and have been named to the Pro Bowl twice. I've had a great time for the past thirteen years earning a living playing a kid's game. I've enjoyed the fruit of my success in the National Football League.

But all of that would mean nothing to me if it weren't for the fact that I can use that platform to lift up the Lord Jesus Christ before people. I'm committed to doing just that, and I'm committed to relying on God to help me endure the tests that are before me.

That has been the key to my success in life, and I know it will work for you too!

## CHAPTER ONE

## WE'RE NUMBER ONE!

# BRINGING THE LOMBARDI TROPHY HOME

There is no higher professional honor for a National Football League player than to play in and win the Super Bowl. It's the goal of each and every player on all thirty teams.

As a member of the Green Bay Packers during the 1996 and 1997 seasons, I had the honor of playing twice in the Super Bowl. On January 26, 1997, my Packer teammates and I became the world champions of professional football.

We came into Super Bowl XXXI as heavy favorites to beat the American Football Conference champion New England Patriots and take home the Packers' first Super Bowl championship since 1968, when Green Bay whipped the Oakland Raiders 33–14 in Super Bowl II.

Like every Super Bowl before it, Super Bowl XXXI was the object of an incredible amount of hype. But when the referee blew his whistle signaling the kickoff, none of that mattered. It was time for us to get out there before the 72,000-plus fans at the Louisiana Superdome and the millions watching around the world on television and prove that the Green Bay Packers were the best team in professional football.

## It's Game Time!

Heading into Super Bowl XXXI, the National Football Conference representative had won twelve straight Super Bowls, and early in the game it looked like the Packers were going to continue that streak. We jumped out to a 10–0 first-quarter lead on Brett Favre's touchdown pass to Andre Rison and a 37-yard field goal by Chris Jacke.

The Patriots came back on us quickly though, scoring on a couple of Drew Bledsoe's passes to give New England a 14–10 lead after one quarter. Suddenly, we had a game on our hands.

We retook the lead early in the second quarter on a spectacular 81-yard touchdown pass from Favre to Antonio Freeman. That Super Bowl-record pass play made it 17–14. Later in the second quarter, Jacke kicked his second field goal of the game and Favre scored on a 2-yard run to give us a 27–14 halftime lead.

As big as those plays in the second quarter were to us, the biggest plays were yet to come.

## A Record-Setting Performance

To win a Super Bowl, a team needs players who can make big plays, who can step up and deliver when the game is on the line. We had several players like that on the 1996 Packers, and two of them stepped up big-time in Super Bowl XXXI.

Curtis Martin, the Patriots' second-year running back and a Pro Bowl player in each of his first two seasons, brought New England to within a touchdown on an 18-yard touchdown run to make it 27–21. At that point, the game everybody thought would be another NFC rout was up for grabs.

It was time for someone to step up, and that someone was Desmond Howard, our kick return specialist. Desmond, who would go on to be named the game's most valuable player after amassing 244 total return yards, gave us another two-touchdown cushion late in the third quarter with a Super Bowl-record 99-yard kickoff return. Desmond fielded Adam Vinatieri's kickoff at the 1-yard line, burst through the center of the return team's wedge, then faked out Vinatieri, the last player with a chance to get him. Desmond's return, along with a 2-point conversion pass from Brett Favre to Mark Chmura, gave us the 14-point lead.

At that point, a little more than twelve minutes separated the Packers from the goal we'd worked for all season long. We led the New England Patriots 35–21 late in the third quarter, and now it was up to our NFL-leading defense to keep Drew Bledsoe, Curtis Martin, and their Patriot teammates out of our end zone.

We kicked off to the Patriots, who were now in a position of having to score immediately in order to give themselves a chance. They had a huge hill to climb and not much time to climb it.

## Making My Contribution

There isn't a player in the NFL who doesn't dream about making the big play in the Super Bowl. We all want to throw the key pass, make the clutch catch, or turn in the big defensive play. I'm no exception.

There were plenty of opportunities for players to make those plays in Super Bowl XXXI. However, none of those opportunities was mine. No, I didn't mess up. I didn't make a boneheaded play that made me the subject of who knows how many replays on television. It's just that there weren't many plays run my way. I didn't have an interception and I didn't cause or recover a fumble. I was one of the cogs in that awesome machine known as the Packer defense.

But I had the privilege of making a huge contribution to the cause, a contribution that never showed up on the stat sheet.

Just before Desmond Howard's touchdown, I could see that Reggie White, our All-Pro defensive end, was struggling. The man who, along with Brett Favre, had been our leader all season long was tired. He'd given this game everything he had, and he was gassed. He didn't have much left.

At the same time, he knew it was time to step up and be counted.

"Gene, I've got to make some plays," Reggie panted. "I'm trying to get into it. Man, I gotta do something. I gotta get goin'!"

Reggie White, this six-foot-five, three-hundred-pound mountain of a man, was looking to me for encouragement. I knew better than to give him the typical pep talk. "You're the man!" wasn't going to work with this massive man of God. He knew that his strength came from Jesus Christ. It also wasn't going to work for me to talk to him about technique or to tell him what he needed to do on the next play. Reggie knew what he needed to do. Now he was looking for the strength to get it done.

I looked at him and did what he'd done for me countless times during the 1996 season and throughout the play-offs. I quoted a Scripture verse, Isaiah 40:31: "'They that *wait* upon the Lord shall *renew* their strength!'" I shouted to him. "'They shall mount up with wings as eagles! They shall *run,* and not be weary! They shall *walk,* and not faint!'" I kept quoting that verse to him on the sidelines, and as we ran out on the field to begin our next defensive series, I continued to quote it to him.

I knew it was time for Reggie White to be lifted up in this game. It was time for God to help him shine in the game he'd worked so hard to get to, that he'd come to Green Bay to play in in the first place. I knew it was going to happen. Right here, right now.

Reggie White said nothing to me at that moment. Instead, he made Super Bowl history.

Reggie was simply awesome in the series that followed Desmond Howard's touchdown. After Drew Bledsoe completed a short pass on first down, Reggie simply abused Patriots right tackle Max Lane and sacked Bledsoe on the next play. The sack, which came on the second-down play, pushed the Patriots back to their own 22-yard line and set up a third-and-22. With the Louisiana Superdome crowd roaring and my Packer teammates celebrating, I ran up to Reggie and said, "That's right, Reg! God is strengthening you! You're mounting up right now!" But he wasn't done. On the very next play, he again threw Lane aside and sacked Bledsoe to push New England back to the 16-yard line, forcing them to punt on fourth-and-long. For all intents and purposes, Super Bowl XXXI was over. We were the world champions of professional football.

## Let's Get This Over With!

I had a sense of confidence that we were going to win Super Bowl XXXI. I respected New England, and I knew they were capable of beating us if we didn't take care of business. But somehow I knew we were going to win. It's a cliché, but I think it fit the 1996 Green Bay Packers: We truly were a team of destiny.

On the other hand, it's one thing to feel confident that you're going to win, but it's quite another to get it done on the football field.

When the game started, I'd had some nervousness and butterflies, but they went away quickly. With the clock winding down, my nervousness came back. It became more and more clear that we were going to win the game, but I didn't want to start celebrating until the final gun sounded. To me, this would be the highlight of a great career, and I didn't want anyone or anything to mess it up. I'd never been on a team that had won a championship—not in high school, not in college, and not in the National Football League.

We were up two touchdowns as the final few minutes of the game ticked away, but I kept thinking, *Stranger things have happened....*

But nothing strange happened. The Packer defense pitched a fourth-quarter shutout that day, and when linebacker Brian Williams intercepted a tipped Bledsoe pass with fifty seconds left, we knew—I knew—it was over. The Packer offense came out, and Brett Favre took a knee. Now it was official. We were number one!

Finally, the Lombardi Trophy—the symbol of supremacy in professional football—was coming back where it belonged: Green Bay, where a coaching legend, Vince Lombardi, crafted a team that has since been the standard of excellence in the NFL.

## What a Day!

It's hard to put into words the feelings that come with winning the Super Bowl. I felt a mixture of pride in my teammates and what they had accomplished and gratitude to God for allowing me the privilege of playing for the winning team in the biggest football game of the year.

I've always said that success wouldn't mean anything to me if I didn't have someone to share it with. This moment was made all the more special because I was able to share it right then and there with the most important people in my life: my wife, Gia, and my daughter, Brittany, and son, Brandon. As the game's final seconds ticked away, I looked in the stands to spot my wife and kids and to encourage them to come down on the field. Somehow, Gia was able to fight through the crowd, convince security that she was my wife, and get herself and the kids to the postgame press conference.

January 26, 1997, was a special day for me on many levels. After eleven years in the NFL, I got a chance to win a Super Bowl and to celebrate the victory with a group of Packers players and coaches I'd grown to respect and love. I had the added blessing of sharing this day with my wife and kids and a pretty good contingent of family members I'd brought to the Superdome that day.

## The Rewards of Endurance

I started this book with my first Super Bowl because to me it demonstrates the value of endurance, both in my life as a football player and in my life as a man who loves God.

Just getting to a Super Bowl—much less winning it—takes incredible endurance on the part of every player and coach on the team. I don't care how talented a team is, how overwhelming it is on offense or defense, that team isn't going to get there without endurance.

Personally, I would never have had a chance to play in the Super Bowl had I not been able to endure some tough times in my career. Don't get me wrong, it's been a great ride for me. I've had some frustrating times in my career, but overall I wouldn't have missed any of it for anything. I have fond memories of my time as a Seattle Seahawk—even of those seasons where we struggled. But I had to endure eleven years in the NFL in order to have my shot at a Super Bowl championship. It took a great amount of work and personal sacrifice to reach that goal.

That need for endurance didn't stop when I joined the Packers. As the 1996 season wore on, we were being touted more and more as one of the favorites to win the Super Bowl. The team had been on a steady ascent for several seasons, and it was starting to look like *our year.* Believe me, the label of *favorite* is not an easy one to wear, mostly because everybody wants to knock you off. (I'll get to that later when I talk about the 1997 season, when we were the defending Super Bowl champions.)

The rewards for our perseverance, our hard work—our endurance— were great, both from a professional standpoint and from a spiritual one. Yes, we earned the Super Bowl rings and all the prestige that comes with them. But we earned something much more important.

## All for Him

The platform that the men of God on the Packers—myself, Reggie White, Don Beebe, Keith Jackson, and the rest—played for is not for the kudos that winning a Super Bowl gets us. It's not for the money or the fame, either. Those things are nice and we all enjoy them, but our top priority is to glorify Christ in all that we do and say. It's to use our influence—influence we've gotten because we won a football game—to let people know that we are committed to giving Jesus Christ credit for everything we do.

God didn't need the Green Bay Packers to win a Super Bowl in order for his name to be lifted up. God could have been glorified whether we won or New England won. Our prayer that week wasn't that we win the game, or even that we play to the best of our abilities. Our prayer was that he be lifted up in the eyes of the world, no matter what the outcome of the game.

The fine line that I and the other Christian men on the Packers that season walked was being committed to glorifying God in our work while at the same time doing everything we could to ensure ourselves a chance to win the Super Bowl. We all wanted God's name to be lifted up, but we also wanted to win the world championship!

The bottom line for all of us was that we were going to endure whatever happened that season, knowing that it was our decision to allow God to use us that would ultimately lift his name higher. As special as just winning the game is, and as special as it is to share that success with my teammates, friends, and family, that is nothing compared with the opportunity to present my Lord to a lost and dying world. It is my relationship with my Lord that gave me the strength to endure the tests and trials that every NFL player faces on his way to the top.

Make no mistake, it's not easy to win a Super Bowl. It takes hard work, study, and a sense of commitment. Most of all, it takes endurance.

And when I give all that I am and all that I have to Jesus, it makes success all the sweeter!

## CHAPTER TWO

# MY CHILDHOOD IN THE HARTFORD GHETTO

I t takes endurance if you want to accomplish anything—in the kingdom of God or in this world. God has taught me over the years the value of endurance, and he started when I was a child growing up in Stowe Village, a ghetto of Hartford, Connecticut.

It's not that my childhood wasn't a happy one. It was. I had a lot of fun growing up in my neighborhood. Some of the best times I can remember having and some of the best friends I can remember making were right there in Stowe Village.

## An Extended Family

When I talk about my old neighborhood, a lot of people think of dysfunction, broken homes, crime, hunger, and squalor. We had our share of that kind of thing, but it also was a neighborhood that had a lot going for it—particularly in terms of community.

My neighborhood was like a huge extended family, where all the adults looked out for one another's kids and the kids looked out for each another. All the kids in my neighborhood played together, fought together, and worked together.

Most of the families in Stowe Village were like mine. They had a mom and a dad and lots of kids—six or more in most cases. Small families were not the norm, nor were single parents. Almost all the kids in that neighborhood had two parents at home, unless one of them had died.

Most of the families in my neighborhood didn't have much, but they somehow got by. There truly was a bond of friendship in our neighborhood, a true feeling of community.

It was also the kind of neighborhood where the bonds of family were greatly valued.

## Mom and Dad

I always tell people that if I was poor growing up, I didn't know it. Thanks to my parents' resourcefulness, we never went hungry and we were always comfortable.

Now that I'm grown with a wife and children of my own, I look back on what Marcella and Samuel Robinson—my mother and father—did for me with a deep sense of gratitude. It's humbling to me to think about how Mom and Dad took care of me and my sisters and brother. They both worked—Mom for an insurance agency and Dad for a company that installed dashboards in cars—and between them they barely took home enough to get by. There wasn't much left after taxes, rent on our apartment, the car, and food and clothes for four kids. Somehow, Mom and Dad made life good for us.

We kids never had any idea how hard our parents had to work or what they had to do without so we had what we needed. When you're a kid, you just don't realize what your parents do—the sacrifices they make—to get by. All you know is that they take care of you.

To me, that's an amazing example of the value of endurance. Day after day, week after week, year after year, Mom and Dad worked their fingers to the bone for us kids. They could have given up—a lot of parents did—but they stayed with it. They stuck it out through the hard times for us.

Mom and Dad always made sure we had what we needed. And there was one other thing they didn't fail to provide when we needed it: corporal punishment.

## Gettin' a Whoopin'

There wasn't a kid in my neighborhood who didn't feel the sting of his father's belt—and occasionally the sting of his neighbor's father's belt. As kids, we called that "gettin' a whoopin'," and it happened to everybody in Stowe Village. We didn't have time-outs, and the parents in our neighborhood didn't buy into the idea that a spanking will cause their kids to grow up to be criminals or dysfunctional people. If you messed up, you got a whipping. And if you messed up in front of your neighbors, you got a whipping from them, and then one from your own parents when the neighbors told them what you'd done.

The neighborhood grapevine never failed to carry bad news to your parents. All us kids understood the score, and when somebody committed an offense worthy of a whoopin', it was like a small-scale scandal had erupted. It created a lot of peer pressure, because no one wanted to get a whipping. I can still remember my friends looking wide-eyed at someone who was about to bear the punishment for something he'd done, saying, "Oh man, you're going to get a whoopin' when your mom finds out!"

Getting a whipping from my dad or my mom—or somebody else's— wasn't fun, but the pain only lasted a few minutes. I lived through it. The thing that lasted—the thing that every kid in my neighborhood feared—was getting grounded. There was nothing worse in our world than to be grounded and not be able to go outside with your friends. When you were grounded, you had nothing fun to do inside. What made it worse was that all the noise, all the hustle and bustle of kids playing, was going on right outside your window and you could do nothing but sit and listen to it.

Those are the sounds I remember fondly.

## Playing with My Friends

We didn't have a lot of expensive toys when I was a kid. Nobody in our neighborhood had the kinds of things that so many kids have today. That was okay, though. In fact, it was better for us because what we lacked in material goods (remember, we didn't know what we were missing anyway), we more than made up for by being outside playing with our friends.

I remember Mom saying, with just a hint of impatience in her voice, "In or out?" when we would come and go from our apartment. That was an easy answer for most of us. We always preferred being outside. Outside is where things were happening. Outside is where there was a big world for us to explore, where there was an unlimited number of things to do.

A typical kid's day in Stowe Village started early in the morning, when the kids went to school in the winter and out to play in the summer. Sometimes we'd go out with our friends early in the morning and not come home till six hours later (with the possible exception of lunch or a bathroom break). We'd be out playing—having a good time. We played sports of all kinds—football, basketball, baseball, kick the can…if a group of kids can play a game, we played it.

Our bikes were our mode of transportation back then. We would sometimes ride ten to fifteen miles just to get to and from our football or basketball games. We'd tell Mom that we were going to our basketball games and that we were riding our bikes. She'd give us fifty cents for lunch, and we were gone. We'd leave at nine in the morning and get home around four in the afternoon.

The kids in my neighborhood played sandlot football and baseball and playground basketball long before we started playing organized sports. We'd get together, go to the field or court, pick sides, and play. And when we started playing organized sports, we'd go to our league games, then head right back out to the sandlot for a game.

There were no age divisions when we played. In my neighborhood, you played against kids who were older than you. When you were eight, you played against kids who were twelve or thirteen years old. That was true in every major sport—football, basketball, and baseball—in addition to the kids' games we played.

## Learning from My Brother

My brother Samuel was a great athlete. He was a good football, basketball, and baseball player. Although he was just a little over a year older, he was much bigger and stronger than I was. In fact, he was better developed than most kids two or three years older than him.

I was small for my age when I was a kid, and that limited me somewhat when it came to sports. I wasn't big enough or good enough to play basketball on the playgrounds. I always brought the ball, but the bigger kids would always take my ball away from me and play as I watched. I'd sit there watching them play eight or nine games in a row with my ball, with my only opportunity to get on the court in between games, when I'd sneak in and shoot a few baskets before the bigger kids started playing again. Eventually, I got tired of standing there watching and concentrated on playing football with my brother.

Samuel and I played sandlot football together with the kids in our neighborhood and from other neighborhoods. When we were nine and ten, we played against kids who were twelve or thirteen. At that age, a few years' difference is huge when it comes to athletics. The kids I played against were much bigger and stronger that I was, but I was always determined not to let my lack of size get in the way of playing with my brother and friends.

Samuel played quarterback and I was his receiver. He taught me a lot about running patterns and looking for the ball when he threw it. One day, he taught me a lesson in football that I'll never forget. We were playing two-on-two football in a parking lot between a couple of cars, and we were losing. We needed a touchdown to win. We huddled together and he told me, "I want you to go by the Buick Electra 225 and act like you're going on out for the bomb. But I want you to stop really fast, and before you stop, the ball is going to be there. Just turn around and catch it." I did what Samuel had instructed me to do, and it worked. I stopped, turned, and the ball was there. I caught it and got touched.

In our next huddle, Samuel said, "I want you to do what you just did, but this time I want you to go for a bomb." I did what he told me to do. I faked like I was going to stop, then took off. Samuel threw the ball and I caught it for a touchdown. My brother and I met after the play and high-fived each other. Then he said something I've never forgotten: "Don't you forget, Keefy (everybody called me Keefe or Keefy because my middle name is Keefe), it only takes one play to win a game!"

I haven't forgotten that, either. I took that lesson with me to every level of football I've played since then.

## A Sister, a Playmate, an Extension of Mom

My sister Deborah, who is five years older than I am, was the oldest of the Robinson kids, and she was an amazing young woman.

She was athletic and tough. She never played organized sports, but she played football and ran track with my brother and me, and she could beat most of the boys in our neighborhood. She played quarterback when she played football with us, and nobody could tackle her. When they'd try, she'd run them over. She was also fast, and nobody could beat her running. And when it came to getting into fights, Deborah was always there with her brothers, helping out and, more often than not, holding her own against the boys.

Deborah was also an extension of Mom when Mom wasn't home. She took care of us when Mom and Dad were at work. More than anything, Deborah was an enforcer. Using force if necessary, she made sure that Mom's orders were followed to a T. For example, if Mom said we were to have soup for lunch, we had soup, period! Deborah was a sweet and loving sister, but if Mom said to do something, she was going to make sure we did it.

Samuel tried on many occasions to challenge Deborah, and he'd get a beating every time. She'd really mess him up when he tried to buck her authority. She'd grab him by the head and knock him down, and if he tried to get up she'd knock him down again. He'd cry, then he'd do what she told him to do.

Sometimes Samuel would protest, "I'm going to tell Mom!" but Deborah knew that wouldn't get him anywhere. She'd tell him, "You go right ahead and tell Mom. It won't do you any good." It didn't, either. When Samuel tried to plead his case to Mom, she'd look at him and say, "Well, you'd better listen to your sister next time. She's in charge, and you know that."

Renee, the second oldest of the Robinson kids, and I learned a lot from watching what happened when Samuel messed with Deborah, and we didn't want any of that. I didn't want a beating from my big sister, so I kept my mouth shut and did what she told me to do. For me it was, "Yes, ma'am" and "No, ma'am" when Deborah told me to do something.

I said before that Deborah was a remarkable young woman. She was tough, strong, and she didn't put up with nonsense out of her younger siblings. But she also had a tender side, a side I saw come out one memorable day when I was out playing with my friends.

## I'm Chuck Foreman!

All the kids in my neighborhood had players they idolized and tried to emulate. We'd actually pretend to be that player when we played, copying his moves and mannerisms. My brother liked Mercury Morris, the Miami running back during the Dolphins Super Bowl years of the early 1970s. For me, it was Chuck Foreman of the Minnesota Vikings. He was so big, yet so smooth. To me, he was the greatest running back there ever was, and I wanted to be just like him. I always ran around with the football, doing the same kind of spins he did and telling my friends, "I'm Chuck Foreman!"

One day I almost cut my ear off trying to be like my hero, and Deborah kept me out of trouble when it happened.

My brother and I were playing football with some of the neighborhood kids, and on one play Samuel threw the ball long. I ran under it, dove, and laid out to catch it, and when I came down, I scraped the side of my head on the gravel surface we were playing on, cutting my ear badly on a rock.

I jumped up and yelled, "Did you see that catch? That looked just like Chuck Foreman!"

I knew I'd made a great catch. What I didn't know was that my ear was hanging from the side of my head with blood oozing down my neck from the wound. It didn't take my friends long to see what I'd done.

"Ooooh! Keefy, Keefy!" my friends said, wide-eyed. I thought they were showing their amazement at the catch I'd just made.

"Yeah, that's right! You saw that catch!" I said. "Just like Chuck Foreman. I'm Chuck Foreman!"

"Man, look at your ear!" one of my friends said.

I remember thinking that it would have been impossible for me to look at my ear without a mirror, but right about that time, I felt something warm and wet on the side of my head. I reached over and felt the side of my head, then looked at my hand. *I was bleeding!*

"Man, I'm bleeding," I said as I started crying.

"Man, your ear's hanging off!"

It was, too. I had ripped a big chunk of my ear almost completely off. I ran home, the whole time crying and wondering what Mom was going to do to me. "Man, I'm going to be in trouble," I sobbed to myself. "Mom's gonna get me. She told me not to be falling down and getting hurt."

I ran in the front door and called out to my big sister for help.

"Deb! I'm bleeding! I'm bleeding, Deb!"

Deborah looked at my ear and said, "Oh Keefe! I don't know what to do with you," then took me in the bathroom and took a cold, wet rag and some gauze and smashed it against my ear to stop the bleeding.

Eventually the bleeding slowed, but that didn't ease the fear I felt at having to face Mom when she got home. "Momma's gonna kill me," I said to Deborah. "I'm going to be in so much trouble." I was worried almost sick that I was going to be in trouble, but my sister stepped in to ease the blow. When Mom got home from work, Deborah met her at the front door and gently broke the news.

"Ma, I just want you to know Keefe got hurt today. He's okay, but we need to take him to the hospital to get some stitches."

"What did he do this time?"

"Well, he cut his head."

Mom took a look at me, and then she and Deborah took me to the hospital, and the doctor stitched my ear back to my head. Mom scolded me a little, but that was the end of it. Thanks to Deborah, I never got in trouble for getting hurt.

The very next day, I was back out playing football—a little wiser and a little tougher. I wasn't worried about getting hurt again.

I was Chuck Foreman!

## CHAPTER THREE

## ATHLETICS AND ACADEMICS

# ONE AVERAGE FOOTBALL PLAYER, ONE FINE STUDENT

When you think of a National Football League defensive back who is closing in on 50 interceptions, who has started in two Super Bowls, and who has been named to two Pro Bowls, you might think he came from a background where he was a star in high school and a "blue chip" college recruit.

That's true for a lot of NFL players, but not for me. I've always thought of myself as the kind of player who beats the norm, and that is demonstrated in my athletic background. I was a decent high school football player—at least during my junior and senior years—but I wasn't anything special.

I learned a lot about endurance early in my high school football career. I learned that because I never got a chance to play.

## Stuck on the Bench

I played football at Weaver High School in Hartford. Actually, it would be more accurate to say that I played football my junior and senior years, because I didn't play at all my freshman and sophomore years because I was so small. When I went out for football my freshman year, I was five-feet-four-inches tall and a skinny ninety pounds. I was pretty tough for my size because I'd played against bigger kids when I was younger, but that didn't matter once I got to high school.

I always tell people that my coaches didn't let me play that season because they didn't want a lawsuit after I got hurt playing against bigger, stronger kids. I practiced my heart out every day, but come game time, I knew I wasn't going to get in—even if the game was a blowout.

Instead, I watched my brother Samuel play. Samuel was always my hero when I was a kid. I looked up to him because he was so good in every sport he tried. He was a year ahead of me in high school, and as a sophomore he was one of the best players on the team. He was six feet tall and 170 pounds, and he played cornerback. I really admired my brother, and I loved watching him play. But I still longed to play on the same field with him.

Although I never got in the games, the coaches at Weaver High School gave me a uniform and let me dress for the games, so I felt like one of the guys. And I wouldn't quit because I knew I could play. I was small, but I was really aggressive. I got knocked around quite a bit in practice, but I didn't care. I wouldn't back down from the bigger guys, but I was going to have to wait to get a chance to play until I grew some more. In the meantime, there was a sport where I could excel, even if I never gained another pound: wrestling.

## Excelling on the Mat

The great thing about wrestling is that a small kid can be the toughest guy on the team because you compete only against guys your own size. You don't have one-hundred-pound kids wrestling against the heavyweights.

Wrestling is a sport where you need a lot of endurance. You have to make weight, while at the same time keeping up your strength and stamina. Then you have to compete on the mat, and that can require an amazing amount of endurance. Having wrestled myself, I still have a great deal of respect for wrestlers and what they do in order to succeed.

I really excelled at wrestling. I took fourth at the Connecticut state tournament at 107 pounds during my sophomore year. I had moved up several weight classes during my junior year and didn't do as well that season, but as a senior I went undefeated in the regular season, then took third in the state tournament at 147 pounds. The state champion, who was from Enfield, Connecticut, the site of the state tournament, beat me 6–5 in the semifinals. He had a big lead on me early, but I came back on him, falling just short of winning as time ran out. I remember how disappointed I was to lose to him. All season long, including the state tournament, I had destroyed everybody else—including the guy who took second at state that year. I was sure going into the semifinals that I would beat this guy.

## Finally—A Chance to Play

While I was a good wrestler, football was always my passion. Still, it took a lot of endurance on my part before I got a chance to play. By the time my junior year rolled around, I was still small—about five-feet-seven-inches tall and 132 pounds—but I had grown big enough that the coaches finally felt comfortable giving me a shot.

I think the thing the coaches saw in me was that I had a lot of endurance and courage. I was also a good athlete and in great shape. I was fairly fast, and I could run all day long. On top of that, I played as if I had no concern for my body. In practice, I'd come up from my safety position and really pop guys who were fifty pounds heavier than I was. I got knocked around sometimes, but I also did my share of hitting. I didn't care if I got the worst of it on one play; I'd come back on the next play and do my best to knock somebody down.

I finally got my chance when Brian White, one of the assistant coaches at Weaver High School and a former player in the National Football League, noticed me. Coach White saw this little guy who was out there laying hits on guys who were half again his size, who wouldn't back down, and who never stopped playing hard. That impressed him.

"I like that kid," he said to our head coach, Lavelle Hill. "He's good. He's got a lot of heart. I want to make him a free safety."

Fortunately for me, the head coach agreed. After all that time of sitting on the bench, I finally got my shot. I made the most of it. I started at free safety my junior year, and I played pretty well. I had 6 interceptions and more than my share of tackles. I wasn't afraid to come up and hit people. I had a great time, and what made it even better was that I finally got a chance to play with Samuel on the varsity football team.

We had a lot of talent my junior year, but the talent didn't translate into a great season. We finished 5–4, losing some close games that we should have won. As a team, we just didn't know how to finish close games. Remember what my brother told me about how it takes one play to win a game? Well, we never seemed to get that one play, and we didn't seem to understand that you have to play a full four quarters in high school football.

## Enduring a Tough Senior Year

My senior year, closing out strong in close games wasn't a problem—mostly because we got blown out most every week. Most of the top players from my junior year, including Samuel, had graduated, leaving us short of talent and experience. We finished 1–8, winning our last game of the season 24–8 over Hartford Public High School. Prior to that last game, we had scored only 16 points all season.

I had a great senior year. I had grown to about 147 pounds by then, which still was small by high school football standards. I had become not just a confident football player but a ferocious hitter. I would come up and lay people out. I finished the season with 5 interceptions and more than 100 tackles.

Obviously, we didn't go anywhere when my senior season ended. I would have loved to have played on a winning team my senior year, but I was prepared to settle for being named the most valuable player on the team. I was just sure that I was going to get it. After all, I had led the team in tackles and interceptions and had been the leader and captain of our defense.

I waited through our annual awards banquet to be named MVP. Our coach during my senior year, Wilbur Jones, made his presentation and talked about his players. Then he made the announcement. "The most valuable player...he's done a great job...an outstanding leader and a captain..."

I thought, *Okay, I was the captain of the defense, so it must be*... and I started to stand up.

"...Gary Bell!"

I didn't want people to know about my disappointment or that I thought I was going to win the award, so I continued to stand and just started applauding with the rest of the people at the banquet. As far as anybody knew, I was giving my man Gary Bell a standing ovation!

I was hurt that I wasn't named most valuable player of the Weaver High School football team my senior year. Since then, though, I've looked back on that time in my life as an example of what can happen when you choose to endure tough times and persevere, even when things aren't going your way.

I could very easily have given up on football during my freshman and sophomore seasons. There isn't a football player at any level of play who hasn't known somebody who gave up because they weren't getting their chance to play. There were times when I wanted to quit, when it seemed like I was wasting my time. I couldn't do that, though. I loved football too much to give up. I knew I could play, and I chose to endure some discouraging times until I got my chance.

It happened for me, too. And once my senior season in football was finished, it was time for me to figure out my next step in life.

## What Next?

I wanted to go to college when my senior year at Weaver High School was finished. I wanted to play college football somewhere. The problem was, there wasn't one college program that had taken so much as a look at me— not even the small colleges. It was the same old problem for me: I was too small. I'd had a good senior year, but my size, combined with the fact that I played on a horrible team, kept me off of anybody's recruiting list.

I was going to have to make another way for myself.

Fortunately, I'd always made schoolwork a priority. I was an outstanding student in high school. I got almost straight A's, and I'm not talking about basic courses, either. I took the tough courses in math, science, social studies, English, and history. I never made a big distinction between academics and athletics. By that I mean that I was a good student and a good athlete and competitive with others in both areas. I actually had fun studying and getting good grades.

I was named to the National Honor Society. I hung around with people a lot of other students didn't consider cool—the brains—and I always competed academically with them. I was third in my class my senior year, behind Richard Benjamin and Byron Patton, both of whom were also good athletes and in the National Honor Society. All three of us competed academically and athletically. Although we didn't talk about it much, we were always trying to outdo each other in the classroom. Each of us would check on how the other was doing.

When I look back on my high school years, I'm grateful to God for bringing into my life people with whom I could compete in the classroom. It's hard to say if having them there helped me get better grades, but I know having them there kept me sharp and gave me motivation to get the best grades I could possibly get.

That, as it turns out, was my ticket to college.

## Where Will I Go?

I knew I wanted to go to college after I graduated from high school. The questions were, which college and how would I pay for it? I soon found out that the great thing about getting such good grades in high school was that there were people and colleges out there who were willing to give me money to go to school.

I went to one of those college fairs at my high school where I talked to representatives from different colleges including Colgate University, a liberal arts school in the upstate New York town of Hamilton. I was a good student, but I was also a kid who enjoyed being a wise guy, so I said to him, "Colgate? I don't want to go to a toothpaste school! Get outta here!" I asked the representative to send me an application to Colgate, and although I had smarted off to him, he took care of it. The application soon arrived in the mail.

I filled out the application to Colgate, as well as applications to Brown University and the University of Connecticut. I was accepted to Colgate and

UConn and turned down by Brown. My decision on which college to attend was a no-brainer. Colgate offered me a scholarship, and that, combined with a couple of scholarships I'd already been offered, would nearly cover the costs of attending.

Soon, all the paperwork had been done and all the contracts signed. I was on my way to college at Colgate University.

There was no mention about football in any of the paperwork I had signed to get into Colgate. As far as anybody knew, I was coming to school just to study computer science. That plan changed quickly, though.

## Playing College Football

When Colgate University accepted me and awarded me an academic scholarship, they, like other colleges I'd looked at, had no idea that I had played high school football. The coaches at Colgate had no idea who I was or that I had any interest at all in playing college football.

I thought about playing at Colgate when I first arrived at the campus for an orientation in the early summer of 1981. One day during that time, I got all the extra motivation I needed to come out for the team.

I met several of the football recruits, including a guy named Frank Gordon, who had been recruited to play fullback for Colgate. Somehow we got into a conversation about football, and he turned his attention on me—a 165-pound freshman with the funny-sounding New England accent.

He asked me, "Do you play football?"

"Yeah, I play."

"Well, I'd run your little butt over."

"You'd run me over?"

"Yeah! Over and over. Now get outta here. You talk funny anyway."

I was never one to back down from a challenge like that. That talk I had with Frank lit a fire under me. I was going to prove him wrong.

The next day I knocked on football coach Fred Dunlap's office door and poked my head inside to inform him that I wanted to play football for Colgate. Coach Dunlap and his staff were having a meeting, which I interrupted to ask them if I could come out for the team.

"Hi. My name is Eugene Robinson, and I'd like to come out for football."

Everybody in that room looked at me like I was out of my mind. Finally, Coach Dunlap said, "Well, we already have our slots filled with recruiting, so we'll have to get back to you."

"Okay!" I said, and left.

I don't know if the Colgate coaching staff had taken me seriously that day, and I don't know if they ever would have gotten back to me. After all, what they saw when I walked into that office to talk to them about playing football was a gangly 165-pound freshman who, as far as they knew, had no idea what it took to play college football.

One day, though, I got the break I needed. I was playing catch in the gym with one of the guys on the football team, and one of the assistant coaches came out of the football office and was walking through the gym just as the guy threw a high pass that was near the basketball rim. I jumped up above the rim and caught it with one hand and came back down. The coach turned around and walked back into the football office and told the other coaches that it would be a good idea to give me a shot.

About a week later, another one of the coaches approached me and said, "We want you to come out for football," then told me what I had to do to get started. That was just the invitation I'd hoped for.

Of course, I accepted it!

## Making an Impression

Those who played high school football but never in college—even at a relatively small school like Colgate—have no idea how much of a step up that is in the level of play. The guys who end up playing collegiate football are the stars in high school, the cream of the crop. They're the biggest, the fastest, the smartest, the highest jumping, and hardest hitting players at the high school level.

I don't know if I was just too naive to realize what I was getting myself into, or if my sense of courage overwhelmed the kind of fear and nervousness I should have felt when I first stepped on the practice field at Colgate. I wasn't afraid of anybody on the field. These guys were bigger, faster, and meaner than anybody I'd played against in high school, but I didn't care about that. My attitude was that if somebody could beat me, fine! I wasn't afraid to go head-to-head with anybody.

I played cornerback in college, and I remember well when I first came out for the team being assigned to cover Colgate's top receiver. Again, I wasn't intimidated or worried that he'd beat me. I just worked as hard as I could to cover him. One other thing—I shut him down. I was giving him fits all day long, knocking passes away and putting him on the ground. I got the coaches' attention, too.

I made the varsity team my freshman year at Colgate, but I never played. We finished 7–3, but I didn't contribute a thing. I played on the junior varsity team, where I had a great time and a great season. I scored a couple of touchdowns on punt returns and had several interceptions. I wanted to play on the varsity, but, just like I had my freshman and sophomore years in high school, I would have to be patient and wait for my opportunity.

There was another similarity between my freshman year in high school and in college: I wrestled. I didn't go out for wrestling, but I spent some time at the team's practices. I hadn't planned on going out for wrestling when I first went to Colgate, but I was hanging around the wrestling room after football practice one day, feeling a bit of nostalgia as I watched the Colgate team practice. I started talking with some people there, and I told them I had wrestled in high school and that I'd done very well at the Connecticut state tournament. I got a chance to wrestle one the team's top wrestlers, and I beat him. I started to think that I could have a future in collegiate wrestling, then I realized that I wouldn't have time to play football, wrestle, and keep my grades where I wanted them to be. Colgate cut the wrestling program after that season anyway. There was no decision for me to make. I concentrated on academics and football. And when my sophomore year rolled around, I started to get some playing time.

## Sophomore Year Frustration

As my freshman year in college ended, I continued to grow and to become more fluid and confident as a football player. I believed, heading into my sophomore year, that I would have a great year. I had played in Colgate's spring game—an intrasquad scrimmage held near the end of the school year—and had 3 interceptions and several tackles. I just knew I would be playing a huge role on the team the following season.

It didn't happen, though. The coaches recognized that I'd improved as an athlete, and I started to get some playing time. I played special teams and got some spot play on the regular defense. I felt good that I was progressing, but I was also frustrated at what I perceived at the time as a bit of injustice.

I was playing behind a guy who, frankly, wasn't a very good player. The only time I got in the games was when the starting corner played poorly. When I got in the games I played very well. One game in particular—a game against Boston University, which we had to win to have a shot at going to the NCAA Division 1-AA play-offs—stands out. I'd started the game on the bench, but the starter was getting lit up by the Boston receivers—Paul Lewis and Billy Brooks, who later had a long, successful career in the NFL. My teammate could do nothing to stop either one of them.

As the game went on, I felt more and more frustrated that I wasn't playing. I could hear my father in the stands, yelling, "Put my son in the game! I didn't come out here to watch him on the bench." Finally, in the middle of the third quarter, the Colgate coaches sent me in to play left cornerback. This was easily my best game in college up to that point. I spent most of the time I was on the field covering Billy Brooks, and they couldn't go to him as easily as they had before. I knocked the ball away from Billy several times and made 6 or 7 tackles. I even put one of their running backs out of the game when I tackled him.

We ended up winning that game, and that helped us toward a spot in the 1-AA play-offs. Personally, I believed that I was on my way, that I would be starting the following week.

Again, it didn't happen. The next game I was right back on the bench.

Some of my teammates were asking me why I wasn't in the game. I didn't have any answers. I just knew I was frustrated. I felt like I was being unfairly and unjustly treated. It really got to me, but there was nothing I could do about it.

We finished 8–4 in 1982, my sophomore year, and finished the season with a play-off loss to Delaware. It felt good to be part of a winning program, but it was still tough being kept on the bench—especially when I believed I was a better football player than the guy I backed up.

Although I didn't enjoy that little trial during my sophomore year, I can look back on it now and see that it was good for me. It taught me a lot about endurance and patience, about hanging in there even when you think you're not getting a fair shake. It also humbled me.

I don't know why I was kept on the bench my sophomore season. At that time, I wondered if it wasn't because I was a black kid from a predominately black school trying to play for a predominately white college. I've realized since then that it could also have had something to do with the fact that I wasn't recruited to play for Colgate. Unlike many of the players on the team, some of whom had influential alumni as parents, I wasn't one of the coaches' picks as a player. I had to ask to come out for the team.

I learned that there will be times in my life when I'm not treated fairly—at least not what I consider fairly. I learned something about being patient and waiting for my turn to be elevated.

That's exactly what happened the following season.

## Getting Promoted—Then Slowed Down

I endured the frustration of my sophomore year and refused to become disenchanted with football. I loved the game as much as ever, and I was determined to come back for my junior year and work my way into the starting lineup.

I continued to grow bigger and stronger during the off-season, and when practice started I was named to the starting lineup for the 1983 season. I had a great start to my junior season, but it would be a season cut short by an injury.

We were playing our fifth game of the season against Holy Cross. Crusaders' running back Gill Fenerty got loose on a run and was headed down the sideline. I got a bead on him and was closing in to make the tackle, and just as I got to him, the Holy Cross fullback blocked me low, and my ankle, which was planted, gave way. *Pop!* I had a broken fibula and a dislocated ankle in my right leg. I tumbled to the turf, then tried to get up and walk. I had the adrenaline flowing, and I thought I was going to be okay. I stood up and flopped back down. *I can't believe this,* I thought. *Mom and Dad are here, and now I've broken my leg.*

It seemed like a bad turn of events for me. I'd finally gotten my chance to play college football, and before the season is half over, I'm finished. It was discouraging, but in the long run it was the best thing that could have happened.

God had some major work to do in my life, and I needed to slow down before he could do it.

## CHAPTER FOUR

# MEETING JESUS CHRIST

hurch was a big part of my life when I was a kid. Mom and Dad sent my brother and sisters and me to Mt. Olive Baptist Church in Hartford, and I loved it. The things I learned in church sunk in, too. I've always had a great memory, and I had memorized a lot of the Bible and a lot of the things I'd been taught in church.

I talked about God a lot when I was a kid. I used to tell Reggie Powell, a friend of mine back in high school, "I'm going to heaven one day, Reg. You and me—both of us are going to heaven someday. I don't know what it is to have wings and fly, but I'm going to do it." In junior high school and high school, I would tell people, "Jesus loves you," trying to be funny.

I used to do a great imitation of a Pentecostal preacher. I'd joke around and preach: "And Jesus said-ah…" "I don't know about you, but I come to serve the Lord-ah…" I was quite a performer, and I could get people going when I preached. They'd be laughing and yelling "amen!" and "preach it!" People at church used to tell my mother, "Your boy's going to be a preacher, Marcella!"

While I took people's telling me I was going to be a preacher only half seriously, I remember vividly a day late in my senior year in high school when I was told that God would use me. I didn't know how God would use me or when, but I always had a feeling that I would serve God when I got older. This was the first time, though, that what someone said about me being a servant of God took hold of me.

I was selected for my school as the recipient of the Daughters of the American Revolution Citizenship Award. Usually, this award is for women, but somehow I won it for my school. The awards banquet wasn't the most comfortable moment of my life. It was a high-class event where we had tea and crumpets. I was just little old Eugene from the hood. We don't have crumpets in the hood. I didn't even know what a crumpet was! On top of that, I'd won what I considered a girls award, so I was a little embarrassed just to be there.

As the awards ceremony opened, a woman came to the dais to do the invocation. She was an elderly woman in a wheelchair. She delivered the invocation, then was wheeled back to her place in the audience. When the program ended, I prepared to leave. On my way out, the woman in the wheelchair got my attention.

"Young man, come here please," she said. I was always respectful to my elders, so I obeyed. I was more than willing to help wheel her out the door or do whatever it was she needed, but she didn't need any help. She had something to say to me.

"Kneel down here, young man," she said. I bent down and listened attentively as she said, "God wants to use you tremendously, and you need to let him."

I had no idea what she meant by that. I believed her, and it scared me. I'd heard people say before that I would be a preacher, but hearing that never affected me the way this did. I knew that I believed in God, but it scared me to think that he wanted to use *me*.

There was one problem with what that woman at the awards banquet had said to me: I didn't know God. I didn't get to know him until after my junior year in college.

## Meeting God

Looking back on my childhood, I can see a kid with an affinity toward God and his Word. What I can't see—and what didn't exist in my life—is a relationship with Jesus Christ. In fact, I didn't even know what it meant to have a personal relationship with him.

I could convince anybody that I was truly a Christian. I knew a lot about the Bible, and I talked a lot about God. But I didn't *know* Jesus Christ. I went through a childhood of attending church, talking about God, hearing his Word, and I'd gone through two-and-a-half years of college without knowing God. Now, it was time for me to slow down and meet him for the first time. And I would have plenty of time to think about that, because my junior football season ended halfway through, leaving God all the time he needed to bring me into his kingdom.

God used a catastrophic—by football standards—injury to slow me down. The questions I've been asked before are, did God *cause* me to be injured so that I would slow down and pay attention to him? Did he bring about a temporary disaster in my life so that he could save me from an eternity apart from him?

I don't know if God caused my injury, but I've come to know this about him: When he wants to make a change in someone's life, he does it by any means necessary. I have never been one to get into theological debates about whether or not God causes bad things to happen to us so that we'll slow down and pay attention. The bottom line is that he used my injury to arrest my thinking and change my heart so that I could get right with him.

## Mixed Motives

When my junior year ended, I started going to church with the woman who would one day become my wife, Gia Michaud. I have to be honest and tell you that I didn't initially go to church because I was searching for God. I just wanted to impress Gia and let everybody at her church know she was with me.

I met Gia for the first time at a Halloween party at Colgate University in 1982. She was a freshman at Cazenovia College, which wasn't far from Hamilton. Actually, we had met before—kind of. After we met, Gia and I soon realized that our paths had crossed when we attended the same grammar school—Fred D. Wish Elementary School in Hartford. We were from the same neighborhood. When I was first getting to know her, Gia told me about two little boys in our neighborhood who would pick on her mercilessly. She remembered one of the boys because she knew his sister. His name was Hector

Rodriguez…a friend of mine from grammar school. Gia's other tormentor was a mischievous little black kid whose name she couldn't remember.

"Did you used to wear two long braids and did your mom used to come and wait for you after school?" I asked Gia.

"Yeah. How did you know that?"

"It was me. Hector and I used to beat up the girls every day after school and chase them home."

Now Gia knew something about my past: I had been a prankish kid who liked to pick on the girls. But there was something else she soon realized about me. Even though I knew some things about God and the Bible, Gia knew I wasn't a Christian. She knew I was an example of someone who had the head knowledge *about* the Savior, but not the heart knowledge *of* the Savior. Gia had been a Christian since the age of thirteen, and it didn't take her long to realize that I wasn't the genuine article.

I didn't realize it at the time, but Gia considered me more of a friend during the first year we knew one another. I thought of her as my girlfriend, but she wouldn't take that step with me. She couldn't. She had a serious, growing relationship with Jesus Christ, and getting serious with me would have been a compromise she wasn't willing to make. She was willing to be my friend, to visit me at Colgate, to talk to me on the phone, and to spend time with me. And she was willing to take me to church. It was there that God first reached down and got hold of me.

My lack of a personal knowledge of Jesus showed in how I lived. First of all, I had a foul mouth. I'd swear and take the Lord's name in vain. I tried to keep a lid on the profanity when I was around her, but when you're used to talking that way, it's bound to come out. Gia let me know that my taking the Lord's name in vain offended her.

Being around Gia made me think. As the school year wore on, I thought more and more about God and what he wanted from me. In the process, my ideas about him were challenged.

## A Time of Testing

As I pondered what God wanted from me, I endured the questions of my friends, particularly my black friends. I remember well a conversation I had where I was asked how I could consider a "white" religion.

"How can a black man serve a white God?" my friend asked me. "How can you serve a white man's God when we've been subjugated and enslaved for four hundred years?

"Religion is nothing more than the opiate of the people. It's nothing more than a drug that the white man uses to keep the black man down."

Another friend of mine, a football player by the name of Lenny Buddington, said the same kinds of things to me. When he challenged me, I somehow knew I had to stand up for what I believed in, and my church-attending background started to come out.

"Lenny, let me ask you something," I challenged him. "Just say for one moment that I'm right and you're wrong. Say that everything you've heard about Jesus is true. Let's say that he did die for you and that the only way you can get to heaven is through him."

"Yeah, okay!" he said, angrily.

"Now, we both die, and I've accepted him and you haven't. What do you say to God as you're standing before his throne? What do you say *right now* to God, Lenny? Because the only question I think he's going to ask you is, 'Have you accepted my Son?' Are you going to look at him and say, 'Well, God, I grew up in the United States of America, and for four hundred years the black man has been a slave to the oppressive white society, and because of that I've built up a resistance toward white people and toward their religion. For that reason, I want to distance myself from anything that might be "white"'?

"That's sounds pretty dumb to me. That just sounds like bitterness. God wants to know if you know his Son, who died for you, and all you've got to talk about is what somebody else has done to you.

"I'm not talking about what somebody else has done to you, I'm talking about what Jesus has done for you. It's something to think about, man."

My friend and I left our conversation that day without settling anything in his mind. I continued to think a lot about Jesus as the school year drew to a close. When June rolled around it was time for me to head back to Hartford. It was at that time that God claimed me as one of his own.

## Decision Time

I started attending church with Gia at North End Church of Christ in Hartford. It was then that God removed the blinders from my eyes that kept me from coming to know him personally. I started to hear the gospel of Christ again—for the first time!

It was incredible to me how the preacher at Gia's church, James Lane, seemed to be talking directly to me. It was as if he knew more about my life than I did. I started to wonder if Gia had been telling him about me and the way I had been living, and he was preaching to me personally.

Because of my background, I knew I was a sinner. But I heard something at church that blew my mind. Pastor Lane said that my lifestyle *offended* God. Furthermore, I was going to hell because of the way I was living. It was as if he was looking me in the eye and saying, "Eugene Robinson, you are living a life that is an offense to the living God, and because of that, you, Eugene Robinson, are going to hell forever."

There was good news for me in Pastor Lane's message. There was a way I could escape God's punishment for my sin. One way. It was through accepting God's gift of salvation through faith in Jesus Christ, who died on the cross to pay for every rotten thing I had ever done. To escape that punishment, I needed a *personal relationship* with Jesus Christ. He had to be *my* Savior and *my* Lord.

That was a new concept to me. I knew about Jesus Christ dying for the sins of the world and that he was the way to God. But the idea of having a personal relationship with him was a new one on me. I'd either never heard that before, or if I had, I couldn't comprehend it. It may be that I'd been told hundreds of times in church that I needed a personal relationship with Christ, but the Holy Spirit hadn't previously illuminated that fact for me.

On June 10, 1984, James Lane preached his Sunday morning message, then closed with his invitation. "Does anybody want to accept Jesus Christ as their personal Lord and Savior?" I jumped out of my seat, raised my hand, and ran down the aisle toward the altar. "Yeah, I do! I want Jesus!" I cried out. I didn't care if I looked silly standing up and running down the aisle. I didn't think about the fact that Gia, this beautiful young woman who had a hold on my heart, was watching what I was doing. All I knew was that I wanted to know Jesus Christ and to live the way he wanted me to live. I wanted all that—TODAY!

I made my way to the altar, and Pastor Lane prayed with me as I received Christ into my life. As I finished praying with Pastor Lane, I felt a deep sense of peace, a sense that I was right with God. I knew beyond any doubt that this decision was just the beginning of incredible change in my life.

I had become a new man with a new purpose in life. I became a man who personally knew the Savior.

## New Things Have Come

Nothing will change your perspective like coming to know Jesus Christ. When I first got saved, I was in love with God. Everything I said and did and thought was about him.

I was like a sponge when it came to the Word. I couldn't get enough. I wanted to know everything there was to know about God and my relationship with him. I even sought out training in the things of God.

I knew I needed a strong foundation in my faith before I headed back to school. One day in church, I stood up and said, "I want a man here to disciple me before I go back to school. I want someone to get with me to get me solid and ready to face school. Who will do that for me?" A man named Astin Dakers (everybody called him "Austin") stood up and volunteered to disciple me.

I submitted myself to Astin's teaching for the rest of the summer. He taught me the basics about faith and the Word. Astin was very sound in his knowledge of the Word of God, and he was a methodical teacher. I always understood Astin's teaching. Whether he talked about salvation, baptism, or the filling of the Holy Spirit, I understood him. To this day, I can still remember Astin's teaching.

Astin taught me the importance of sharing my faith with other people, and he showed me how to do it. Many times that summer, he'd say, "Let's go walk the street and tell people about Jesus," and we would go do street ministry in Hartford—just walking around and looking for people to tell about Jesus Christ.

I was so focused at that time on my relationship with Jesus Christ that very little else mattered. Even Gia took a backseat to God at that time. I never forgot about her. I still called her from time to time, but I didn't see her much. She later told me that she found it upsetting that she brought me to church hoping to see me give my life to Christ, only to lose me—at least temporarily—when my focus turned to him. I'm happy to say that God didn't take me away from Gia—or Gia away from me...at least not permanently.

When I first came to know Jesus, there were only a few months before I returned to Colgate, a place where I would enjoy incredible spiritual growth and endure some amazing trials.

## New Friends, New Experiences

Nothing in the Bible promises us that following Jesus Christ will be easy. The Word says in many places that being a Christian is anything but easy. It promises us persecution, testings, trials, and other tough times. But it also promises us great rewards if we endure these things.

When I got back to Colgate for my senior year, I had to endure all sorts of challenges—from my teammates, my friends, and from professors. But it was a time where God brought people into my life who were incredible sources of encouragement, as well as challenges in my own walk with God.

Before I got saved, I was what you might call a "party guy." I didn't drink or do drugs, but I was the kind of guy who schemed on the ladies. When I came back to school, I wasn't like that anymore. I just didn't want to be. I didn't want to party, and I didn't want to chase girls. I wanted my life to please God.

Everything was different for me when I got back to Colgate for my senior year. Even the people I spent my time with. That year, I hung out with the

THE BIGGEST DECISION OF MY LIFE

people I had said before I would never hang out with—the goofy people. You know...the Christians.

I had a core group of four Christian friends I started spending time with: Orlando Crespo, Nancy Rodriquez, Dawn Zordragger, and Scott Deerwester, a computer science professor at Colgate. This group offered me the encouragement I needed to grow in my faith and to endure the tests that were yet to come.

I first met this group one day when I left the computer room at Colgate to head for football practice. Halfway to practice, I turned and went back to the computer room. I had no idea why I was heading back, only that I needed to go there. I walked into the computer room and looked around, then went to Scott Deerwester's office, where he and Dawn Zordragger were talking, and said, "I don't know why, but I'm supposed to be here."

Scott and Dawn looked at me, then at one another, and smiled. They knew why I was there. The very moment before I had walked in, they had been talking about starting a Friday morning prayer group and about who should join that group.

"We know why you're supposed to be here!" Scott said. "You're supposed to pray with us on Friday mornings."

When I walked into Scott's office that morning, I didn't know him—at least not personally—or Dawn. Neither of them knew who I was, and they certainly didn't know I was a believer. They were just two followers of Christ praying for direction in how they should ask for revival on the Colgate University campus. God answered that prayer on the spot when I walked into the office and interrupted them.

We met every Friday morning after that, and we prayed for revival. God sent it, too. He sent it to all five of us individually, then moved us out into our own worlds so that we could propagate the gospel of Jesus Christ.

## Locker Room Testings

When I returned to Colgate for fall football practice in August of 1984, I was a different person from the one whose season was cut short the year before by the leg injury.

When I got saved the previous June, I had put my rehabilitation exercises aside and concentrated on spiritual matters. I didn't do much rehab. When practice started, I felt some pain, but it wasn't anything serious. It was just stiffness and soreness, and it soon passed.

What didn't pass, though, was my desire to bring the Word of God to my teammates. It wasn't easy to do, but nothing that's worth doing is. I remembered after I got saved how my teammates and I used to talk about God the previous two years. We talked about him the same way we talked about current events or politics. We talked about our theories on God, the Bible, and Jesus. It was different now that I was a Christian. I was no longer talking about God like a historical figure. Now, I was talking about someone with whom I had a personal relationship.

I had always been an outgoing person who enjoyed being with my teammates—talking to them, joking around with them, and laughing with them. That didn't change when I got saved. I still had good friends on the Colgate football team, but now I had a different objective in those friendships: I wanted my teammates to know what had happened to me, and I wanted them to know they could have the same thing I had.

The conversations I had with my teammates were often positive, and many of them had questions for me. Other times, however, my statement of faith created conflict for me. I remember well a discussion I had with a good friend of mine, Frank Gordon, the same guy who motivated me to come out for football my freshman year by telling me he was going to run me over. There were eight or nine of us football players having a discussion about God. I told the guys what I believed: That Jesus Christ had died for all our sins, and that he was the only way any of us would see heaven. That statement upset Frank, and he challenged me on it. He said, "You're telling me that somebody like my father—who is a good and decent man who loves his wife and children—is going to hell if he doesn't know Jesus Christ! Is that what you're telling me?"

The room went dead silent as everybody waited to hear my response. I imagine they all wondered if I would back down or if I would stick to what I had said earlier. I looked at Frank and calmly said, "I will say this: If you don't know Jesus Christ, you will not be in heaven. If your father doesn't know Jesus Christ, then, yes, he won't go to heaven. He'll go to hell. That's what I'm telling you, Frank."

Before I was saved, I always wanted to fight Frank because he was bigger and thought of himself as tough. I didn't want to fight him now. I just wanted him to understand what I was telling him—that Jesus Christ was the only way for anybody to get to heaven. I wanted him to know that Jesus made a way for any of us who will respond to him in faith to spend eternity with him in heaven.

Frank looked at me, his lip trembling and his body shaking, and he stood up. Everybody watched and waited to see what Frank, who stood six-foot-three and weighed 220 pounds, would do or say next. He just looked at me—nose to nose, eye to eye.

I couldn't back down. I had to stand my ground—not to show Frank and my teammates that I wouldn't be intimidated, but to let him know just how serious I was about wanting him to understand that knowing Jesus was the only way to heaven.

"Frank, you don't have to go to hell. Nobody has to go to hell," I said. "Hell wasn't designed for you in the first place. But the Bible says that if you don't have a personal relationship with Jesus Christ, then you choose to pay for your sins by yourself, and it takes eternity in hell to pay for your sins."

Eventually, that conversation ended and everybody went their separate ways. Unfortunately, Frank Gordon never brought up the subject of God with me again. He was a friend of mine, so he didn't avoid me, but we never talked about God again—at least not with the seriousness we had before.

## Religious Testings

As a young Christian—saved only a few months—I came face-to-face with one of the groups that actively recruits on college campuses. It's a cult called The Way International, and it teaches some things that are so heretical that I don't want to give them credence by writing them here.

I came into contact with The Way International through a young man named John, who attached himself to the group of Christians I spent time with. Almost from the time he joined our group, we had conflicts with him. All of us had come from different denominational backgrounds, so we had no problem with small doctrinal differences between us. But there was more to it than that. Soon, I found out some of the things John and his group were trying to push.

I didn't know how to approach John to talk about the problems I had with what he believed. One day, though, as I was going to football practice, I had a chance to talk to him. We talked about some of the things he believed in, but I had to cut the conversation short to go to football practice. After practice, I walked back to my dormitory, and as I approached the front door, I had a feeling that there was something not right going on inside. Somehow, I knew that John was waiting inside for me.

He was, but this time he brought help—a man who worked to recruit college students into his group. As I opened the door, John said to his friend, "There he is! That's the guy I've been talking to you about." John's friend introduced himself and asked if we could talk. "Okay," I said. "But you guys stay right here and I'll be right back."

I ran to my dorm room and got my Bible and came back down. John's friend was sent there to recruit me, but that wasn't going to happen. Not as long as I had the Word of God. God built me up at that moment to stand against something that wasn't of him.

As we started talking, John's friend went over some of the things The Way International believed in. I had very limited experience as far as teaching the Word was concerned, but I was able to find a verse to answer every one of The Way's heresies. When I look back on this moment, I'm sure that God was there, guiding me to the Scripture I needed to counter what they were saying. Every time they came at me with something, I had an answer from the Word.

Finally, realizing that he wasn't getting anywhere with me, John's friend turned to him and said, "Let's go."

After that day, John just disappeared from our group. He was gone for good. He left school, and none of us ever saw him again.

## Preparing the Way

It amazes me to think of the kinds of tests I had to endure as a young Christian in college. It seems to me that the enemy was coming at me with everything he had to get me to question what I believed in. I know that God used the things I endured that final year at Colgate University to strengthen and ground me for what he had ahead for me.

College truly was an education for me in every sense of the word. It prepared me for life in the real world. But it also helped prepare me for the ministry I would later have.

I'm talking about a ministry in the world of professional football.

## A ROAD LESS TRAVELED

# TAKING MY OWN ROUTE TO THE NFL

Talk to most players in the National Football League and they'll probably tell you how stressful and exciting those last few weeks before the NFL draft was for them. Most guys talk to agents, scouts—anybody who can give them a clue as to where they might go.

Players who expect or hope to be drafted pay close attention to the draft, waiting for their name to be called. After the draft, the players sign contracts, the terms of which are determined by, among other things, how high they went in the draft. Then it's time to set about the business of making the team.

That, with a few twists and turns along the way, is how most NFL players come into the league. It didn't happen that way for me, though.

I'm the kind of person who takes a different route to where he wants to go. My entry into the NFL was no exception. To start with, I wasn't drafted. Twelve rounds and more than three hundred picks passed in the 1985 draft, and nobody called my name. A couple of teams had contacted me prior to the draft and said they were interested in taking me with a mid- to late-round pick. In fact, the Pittsburgh Steelers called me the day of the draft and said they would take me in the seventh round, but it didn't happen.

It's not surprising that I wasn't drafted, considering the kind of senior season I had. I had a good but not great year on a mediocre (5–5) Colgate team. I finished the year with 52 tackles and 2 interceptions—not bad numbers, but not the kind of statistics that are going to catch a scout's eye. All that and I played for a relatively small school (Colgate was Division 1-AA, which is a lower level than Division 1-A, where schools such as Michigan, Notre Dame, and Southern California compete).

I didn't get a lot of attention from NFL scouts when I was in college, and the attention I got was mostly when they came to watch our quarterback, Steve Calabria. (As it turns out, Steve wasn't drafted either, except by the USFL.)

Disappointed, you ask? Devastated? Not in the least! As odd as it might sound, I wasn't at all concerned that I wasn't drafted. The thought of playing professional football was definitely appealing to me, but I had fully placed my confidence in God, and I knew that he would make a way for whatever he wanted me to do. If he wanted me in the NFL, then he would make sure I got an opportunity.

I was completely content doing what I was doing, content and focused on Jesus Christ and growing in my relationship with him. Instead of putting out effort to get an NFL contract, I did the things God had put before me. I worked to complete my degree in computer science by applying myself and studying hard, and I worked to continue growing spiritually through prayer, fellowship, and study of the Word.

I was truly living by Jesus' instruction to, "seek first his kingdom and his righteousness, and all these things will be given to you as well" (Matthew 6:33). God gave me "all those things." He gave me more than what I had any reason to expect. In the middle of that busy schedule, God made a way for me to talk to an NFL scout about my future in football.

## Talking to the Scouts

It's a long shot, but there is another route for rookies into the NFL other than the draft. It's called signing as a free agent. A player who goes undrafted can sign with any team he wants. It's not easy to make a team that way, though. Not only do you have to fight through all the obstacles any rookie has to in order to make your team, but you also have to fight the fact that you're not one of the coaches' "main guys," because they haven't invested a draft pick in you.

Immediately after the 1985 draft, I started getting calls and visits from NFL teams. I listened to what they had to say—as long as I could fit them into my schedule. As crazy as it might sound now, I wouldn't deviate from my schedule in order to accommodate a scout. I wouldn't miss a class, a lab, a Bible study, or prayer meeting for a scout. It wasn't that I didn't take them seriously. I had a strong sense of commitment, and I believed that if you had scheduled something with somebody, you honored that appointment. I was so confident in the Lord that I would ask the scouts to schedule my tryouts after class or after Bible study.

I had one scout with the Dallas Cowboys offer me a contract right there on the Colgate campus. It was huge money for a college student, especially back then. "I'm with the Dallas Cowboys, and I can offer you a contract right now," the scout told me, then held out the paper and pen. I wanted to talk to the scout further, but I didn't have time at that moment. "I'd like to talk to you more, but I have a test, then a Bible study," I told him. "If you can be here when I get back, I'd love to talk." The scout looked at me like I was crazy, then left. He wasn't there when I returned.

Finally, a scout came who was willing to work with me to schedule a meeting. His name was Earl Norvedt, and he was with the Seattle Seahawks. Earl called me and asked me if I would be interested in meeting with him over dinner to discuss playing for the Seahawks.

"I'd like to meet with you for dinner," I said. "But I have a Bible study the night you want to meet. If you want to meet me after my Bible study, I can do that."

"Bible study?"

"Yes, a Bible study," I replied. "If you want to come out and watch me or talk to me, that's great, but you'll have to wait until after my Bible study. I'll be done about 8:30, if you want to meet then."

"That will be fine," Earl said, and we made an appointment, then hung up.

When I met with Earl, he showed me pictures of Washington and told me about quarterback Jim Zorn and some of the other Christians on the team. I immediately liked Earl (in fact, he and his wife became good friends of ours). He didn't come at me like a recruiter. He didn't give me a song and dance about how I could help the team, and he didn't make any guarantees. Instead, he talked about how beautiful and livable the Pacific Northwest was and about how I would be given a chance to make the team. That impressed me, and I felt comfortable talking to him.

I decided to go to Seattle to see if the Seahawks were right for me. I hired as my agent Phyllis Freed, the mother of one of my friends. We caught a plane and headed west.

## Checking Out Seattle

The Seattle Seahawks didn't have to do much to win me over to the city. Seattle is a beautiful city in a beautiful setting. The city is built around Puget Sound. To the north, you have the Olympic Mountains, to the east the Cascades, including Mt. Rainier, the tallest peak in the Pacific Northwest. To make it all the more impressive, my visit was in May, and it was a beautiful spring day.

Being a city kid from the East Coast, I had never seen anything like Seattle. I was just in awe of its physical beauty. I remember well the moment when I knew I wanted to make Seattle my home. We were driving over Lake Washington on a floating bridge when I saw a pelican dive into the water after a fish. Right there in the middle of one of the biggest cities on the West Coast, you can see birds hunting for fish! I said, "Man, this is like *National Geographic!*"

Later, after I took care of some presigning business, including my physical, I met with Mike Allman, the Seahawks' director of player personnel, in his waterfront office. As we talked, Mike stood up and said, "Eugene, I just want you to take a look out this window." I looked out the window and saw the snowcapped mountains, the Space Needle, and the water. It was incredible. At that moment I thought, *I want to come here. Even if I don't make the team, I want to stay here.*

I was hooked. I was sold on the city more than the team. I signed with the Seahawks. It was time for me to take advantage of the opportunity God had given me.

## An Open Door

Just before I signed with the Seattle Seahawks, I talked to the defensive backs coach, Ralph Hawkins, and he told me, "Son, if you come here you'll get an honest opportunity. We'll give you a chance to make this team."

"That's all I want," I said.

That was true, too. I knew there were no guarantees. I knew that I could have been cut loose anytime after I signed the contract. I knew that as an undrafted free agent it was an uphill battle for me just to get the coaches' attention, let alone to make the team. The Seahawks were giving me no guarantees, and I wouldn't have asked for any. I just wanted a chance to show them what I could do.

The rest was up to God.

As I went through the process of visiting Seattle and signing with the Seahawks, it became more and more clear to me that God was in the middle of all this. He had to be. I had done nothing to pursue a career in the National Football League. I never went to the NFL Combine, a predraft meeting in Indianapolis for prospects who want to show off their physical skills for the scouts. I didn't have an agent out there pounding on doors for me, either. There's nothing wrong with someone who wants to play in the NFL doing that, but that wasn't the road I was taking.

When I came out of high school, my two dreams were to earn my degree in computer science and to play professional football. That changed when I became a Christian. I hadn't thought about playing pro football. All I thought about was serving God. He was opening a door for me to play professional football. Now, it was up to me to walk through that door.

## Training Camp: An Uphill Battle

Chuck Knox, the coach of the Seattle Seahawks when I first signed with the team, used to say, "Nobody's going to make my team in the minicamp." That proved to be true. I found out that, as a new guy, there was nothing I could do in my first minicamp, which was held in May, to make the team. The minicamp is basically an indoctrination period, where a player gets acclimated to what the team is doing. There is lots of classroom time and short noncontact (no pads) practices.

I worked out with the defensive backs at minicamp. All we did, really, is cover receivers. That gave the coaches an idea of whether or not we could cover. I played at cornerback during my first minicamp, and I played pretty well. I looked forward to training camp, which started in July at Eastern Washington State University in Spokane.

A National Football League training camp is a test of a player's endurance, particularly a *young* player's. Training camp is a lot like boot camp in the military. You can't leave and you have to adhere to a regimented schedule. Training camp is, as much as anything, a proving ground where you decide whether or not you really want to play in the NFL and where you prove to your coaches that you can play. Training camp is demanding, and it was especially tough for me, because I was coming into it as not just a low man on the totem pole, but *the* low man.

The Seahawks already had a quality defensive backfield in strong safety Ken Easley, free safety John Harris, cornerbacks Dave Brown and Keith Simpson, plus reserves Terry Jackson and Paul Moyer. They already had the rookies they wanted because they'd drafted them. I knew that to get the coaches' attention, I would have to shine quickly and make a statement that told the coaches, "I belong here!"

There's a lot of pressure in having to perform well on every play, and that's the kind of pressure I felt at my first training camp. When we ran our defensive drills and our scrimmages, I wasn't the number one guy, so I received a limited number of plays. I knew that when I was on the field, I'd better be prepared to perform well. I knew that I had to quickly grasp the Seahawks' defensive system. That meant that I had to be a student of the game, that I had to be paying attention during the hours and hours of class time at training camp, and that I had to be studying the playbook during those few moments of free time we had at training camp.

Everything I learned in the classroom had to translate to something good on the football field. There's no tolerance for mistakes at that level, especially for a free agent rookie. For draft choices there is a small margin for error, but not for me. I had to do it right every time.

While training camp was a mental and physical challenge, I approached it with confidence. First of all, I had confidence that God was in control and had a plan for me. I knew he'd brought me this far and that he wasn't going to just leave me hanging once I got to camp. While I had to endure a lot of pressure during that first camp, I knew that God was there for me, taking care of me and guiding my steps.

I also felt confident because I knew I could play. I wasn't the fastest player in the Seahawks' camp in 1985, but I could run, cover receivers, and tackle people. That confidence had received a boost in January of the same year when I worked out with the New Jersey Generals, who had drafted me with a late pick in the USFL's territorial draft. I spent three days with the Generals, and I worked out with guys like Hershel Walker, Maurice Carthon, Brian Sipe, and Monty Jackson. After a few days at the Generals' camp they told me they wouldn't be needing my services. I went home—knowing I could play football with those guys.

My first NFL training camp was a challenging experience, but I was ready. I knew that I was smart enough to catch on to Seattle's defensive scheme, and I knew I had the physical ability to play at that level. I just wanted the opportunity to prove it.

## Proving Myself

Rookies coming into NFL training camps have to prove themselves against some of the best football players in the world, and they have to do it right away. When I first came into the NFL, I had to prove myself by covering one of the best receivers ever to play the game.

Steve Largent wasn't big or fast by NFL standards, but that didn't stop him from being one of the best in the business. He ran precise routes, adjusted to the ball, and almost never dropped a ball that was within his reach. He was an amazing football player.

My very first play against Largent was during the week before camp officially opened—when the rookies and free agents arrived. Steve arrived early on his own, to get an early start. Steve Moore, the Seahawks' wide receivers coach, had stopped our scrimmage and told the rest of the receivers, "I want you to watch how Steve Largent runs his patterns."

I lined up on Steve Largent, and as he took off from the line of scrimmage, I jammed him as hard as I could. He tried to step to my inside, and I hit him again. He got outside me, and I was able to use what is called the trail technique, where you trail just behind the guy, then cut to the inside of him. We ran downfield about 13 yards, and Steve cut to the inside—where I was already. Dave Kreig, the quarterback, threw the ball Steve's way, but before it could get to him, I dove and attempted to catch it. I was coming down with it but it came out when I hit the ground.

As I walked back, going to where the defensive backs were gathered, I heard Steve Largent ask one of the other defensive backs, "Who is that guy? Number 41?" When I got back to the defensive backs, one of them said, "Hey, Steve Largent wants to know who you are."

I'd gotten Steve Largent's attention, and I had also caught the eye of some of the Seahawk coaches.

The wide receivers coach complained to Ralph Hawkins, the defensive backs coach, that I had tried to injure Steve Largent. I knew better than that, and Steve Largent knew better. So did Ralph Hawkins.

"He's not trying to hurt anybody," Coach Hawkins said. "He's just trying to make this football team."

From that day on, Steve Largent tried to turn me inside out every time we lined up against one another. Sometimes he got the best of me, but I made enough good plays to keep myself in the running for a job with the Seahawks.

I had a great training camp. I started out playing cornerback, but I was moved around the defensive backfield to the safety position late in the camp. That was fine with me. Knowing all the positions gave me some versatility, and that couldn't have hurt my chances of making the team.

It was just a matter of seeing if the coaches saw it that way.

## Becoming a Person

There's a scene in the Vietnam War movie *Full Metal Jacket* where a United States Marine drill instructor tells his squad of recruits on graduation day, "Today, you are no longer *maggots!* Today, you are *Marines!*"

It's a lot like that for rookies in NFL training camps. When you're a rookie nobody seems to care that you're there. Very few people say anything to you—at least until they're sure you've made the team. Part of that, I think, is because they don't want to befriend someone who's not going to be there long. It's also because you have to earn your place in the hierarchy of the team.

My first season, cornerback Dave Brown—who would later become my mentor and friend—was the only veteran who spoke to me with any regularity, and that was after he signed late in the training camp after a holdout. (Actually, I think that was a break for me because it gave me more snaps at practice, so I could show the coaches what I could do. Once Dave got back, my snaps dropped off to almost nothing.) The rest of the veteran defensive backs had their own little clique. They stuck together, and I can't blame them for that. They were a group of guys who had played together and who would be playing together on the regular defense. They weren't going to let anybody else into their circle until that man had earned his way into the team.

One of the few times anybody from that group talked to me was when Ken Easley—a player I greatly admired from what I had heard about him and from what I had seen in training camp—approached me near the end of training camp and complimented me for my play. Ken always called me "Grange" after Red Grange, who starred in professional football in the 1920s. He called me that, he said, because I moved like one of the old-time football players you see in the archive film clips. "Let me tell you something, Grange," he said. "You've been playing well."

That was all Ken Easley said to me during that whole training camp my rookie year. I felt honored to have a player of his stature—an All-Pro and recipient of just about every defensive player of the year award available during the 1984 season—say that to me.

I enjoyed hearing what Ken had to say to me. The question was, did the coaches feel the same way? Had I made enough of an impression to stick with the Seahawks? I knew I had played well, but I also knew that a lot of guys played well in training camp, only to be cut before the regular season started.

I felt confident that I would make the Seahawks' roster, but I have to admit that I was really nervous the day the final cuts were to be made that late August. A lot of guys were nervous that they would be visited by "the Turk," who on the Seahawks at that time was special teams coach Rusty Tillman. When someone was to be cut, Rusty had the unenviable job of telling that player, "You need to go see the coach. Take your playbook with you." Then the player would walk into Coach Knox's office and hear the we-think-you-have-a-lot-of-potential-but...speech. Then it was good-bye to the Seahawks, and more than likely good-bye to dreams of an NFL career.

I never heard that speech as a rookie with the Seahawks, but there was a moment on the day of the final cuts when I was sure it was coming. I was following James Bowers and Arnold Brown, the two rookie defensive backs the Hawks had drafted that year, on my way to the practice facility. As James and Arnold approached the door of the practice facility, Rusty Tillman stopped them and said something I couldn't hear. He had sent them to talk to the coach and, by the way, take their playbooks, too. As I approached the practice facility, I was sure I was going to hear the same thing. Rusty Tillman looked at me, but instead of telling me to go see Coach Knox, he said, "Come on in, Gene, you've made it," and held the door open for me.

My feelings at that moment were a mixture of relief and joy. As I walked into the practice facility, a bunch of guys—some who before wouldn't have said good morning to me—patted me on the back and said, "Congratulations, Gene! You deserve it!" For the first time since I had been in Seattle, I felt like I was welcomed by the Seahawk veterans.

One player, veteran tight end Charlie Young, refused to congratulate me, but brought me back to reality when he said, "I won't congratulate you yet, son. I won't congratulate you until after the season. Make no mistake, they can cut you any time. They bring in people every Tuesday. Now you have to work even harder to keep your job."

*I'm glad somebody said something to me,* I thought. *I'm glad I know.*

Charlie Young was absolutely right in what he said to me. That I hadn't been cut meant I had a job in the NFL for the opening day of the 1985 season. I still had no guarantees. I was still one bad play, one missed assignment from having my pro football career cut short. And back then, getting cut usually meant the end of your career because that was before the free agency rules that allowed a player to sign with another team when he got cut.

Even though I had made the final preseason cut for the Seahawks, there were no guarantees for me of a future in the NFL. But God had opened another door for me, and I had just poked my head inside that door. He had given me the opportunity to try out for the Seahawks, then he had given me the strength to endure training camp.

Now it was up to me to make the best use of what he had given me.

## BREAKING INTO THE LEAGUE

# MAKING PLAYS—AND MISTAKES—
# AS AN NFL ROOKIE

If there's one thing a young player coming into the National Football League needs if he's going to endure his first season, it's patience.

Heading into my first season in the NFL, I knew that earning playing time was going to be another uphill climb. Starting left cornerback Dave Brown had come back from a contractual holdout, and Keith Simpson and Terry Taylor rotated at the other corner. John Harris was the free safety, and Ken Easley was one of the best—if not the best—strong safeties in the league.

With a group like that patrolling the defensive backfield, I was going to need some breaks to get playing time. I was going to have to be patient and contribute to the team in any way I could.

Fortunately for me, there was a way for young players to break into the league.

## A Foot in the Door

Outside of kickers and a few exceptional return men, there aren't a lot of players who make a big name for themselves on special teams. There are exceptions, of course. Every so often a special teams player comes along who has a knack for making the big plays. For most of us, though, special teams are a way for a player to get a foot in the door into the NFL.

Special teams allow a player to contribute to his team until he shows his coaches that he can be productive on the regular offense or defense. It's not that special teams aren't important. Some of the biggest plays in a game can be made by special teams. A big tackle here or a blocked kick there can mean the difference between winning and losing in the NFL.

I started my career in the NFL playing almost nothing but special teams. I played on the kickoff and punt teams, the return teams, and the extra point team. I made some good plays, and I made some mistakes. And little by little, I got an opportunity to play on the regular defense. I played some on the nickel defense (five defensive backs), and I got some playing time late in the season due to injuries.

## The Ups and Downs of My Rookie Season

While my playing time on the Seattle Seahawks was limited during my rookie season, I was able to make some contributions.

My first interception came against the San Diego Chargers in the Kingdome in our fifth game of the season. I was playing on the weak side in the nickel defense, and the receiver ran a route to the back of the end zone. I read the play, and when Chargers quarterback Dan Fouts threw the ball, I jumped up in front of the receiver and caught it. It was a thrill to get my first interception, especially against a quarterback like Dan Fouts. What made it all the sweeter is that it stopped a Chargers' drive and helped us to a 26–21 win.

My second interception was against Kansas City, and it came when I came in to replace Ken Easley and Paul Moyer, who had both been injured on the same play. I heard one of the coaches yelling, "We need a safety!" and there was no one else to go in. I went into the game, and when Chiefs' quarterback Todd Blackledge saw me, he tried to throw a bomb to wide receiver Stephone Paige. I picked it off and ran it back 47 yards to the Chiefs' 15-yard line to set up a touchdown in our 24–6 win.

While I had some good plays during my first year in the NFL, there were also some moments I would just as soon forget. One of them involved an injury to one of my teammates, an injury for which I was largely responsible.

I was playing on a kick return team against the San Diego Chargers, and I blew a blocking assignment, causing Randall Morris, one of our kick return men, to get hurt. I was supposed to block one player, Woodrow Lowe, but I blocked someone else, giving Woodrow, a punishing hitter who played outside linebacker on the regular defense, a free shot at Randall Morris. He hit Randall hard, and it was obvious Randall was injured. It wasn't that Woodrow Lowe beat me on the play, either. It was worse than that. I simply forgot who I was supposed to block on the return.

All I could hear when the play was over was Rusty Tillman screaming, "Eugene Robinson! Eugene Robinson!" I thought, *Oh man, that must have been my guy.* I went to the sideline and got an earful from Coach Tillman. That wasn't the end of it, though. The next day, Coach Knox, who hadn't spoken to me all season, came up behind me in practice and said, "You play almost nothing but special teams. I would have no problem replacing you. I can get someone to do your job. A word to the wise is sufficient."

I got Coach Knox's point. I knew I couldn't afford any more mistakes. I had to make sure I did it right. Otherwise, I could be out the door—in a hurry.

## Listening, Watching, and Learning

There was an upside to the logjam in the Seattle Seahawks defensive backfield during my rookie season. While I didn't get to play much, I learned by watching some of the best in the business.

I cut my teeth learning from guys on the Seahawks like Dave Brown, Ken Easley, and John Harris—men I respected both on and off the field. They all had something to offer a naive rookie like myself. These were guys who knew how to play the game and who could play at a high level.

In Dave Brown, I had a fundamental, methodical teacher who understood the game. Dave taught me the importance of studying, of preparing by watching game films and studying your opponent's offensive schemes. Dave taught that by example, too, as he was one of the most studious football players I have ever met. He also taught me the value of consistency. He used to tell me, "You've got to make more good plays than bad plays."

Dave Brown also taught me the importance of conditioning. He was ten years older than I was when I was a rookie with the Hawks, but I couldn't keep up with him when it came to running. "Man, do you ever sweat?" I'd ask him.

While I learned a lot about the mental aspect of the game from Dave Brown, I learned about the physical part of it from Ken Easley. Ken taught me the value of not being afraid of anything on the football field. He also used to tell me, "You get to the Pro Bowl by making big hits and big interceptions."

Ken Easley talked the talk, but he also walked the walk when it came to playing fierce, physical football. He tried—within the rules—to intimidate every receiver who played against him. He was labeled as a cheap-shot artist by some opposing players, but I never agreed with that. What I saw in Ken was a football player who would knock a hole in you—legally. I knew from playing with Ken that receivers were flat-out afraid of the man. Many times, I saw receivers cower in front of him, knowing that he was going to lower the boom. I saw many receivers who wouldn't go up for high throws when Ken was around because they didn't want to get leveled. It's called "hearing footsteps" in our business, and Ken Easley was one of the best ever at making that happen.

John Harris wasn't as fast or as hard a hitter as Ken Easley, but he was a great student of the game. When we came into a game against a certain team, John was the one who always knew what the opposing players liked to do. On the field, it seemed like he had a sixth sense when it came to reading plays. It was like he knew what was going to happen before it happened. I'd see him make a play, a play nobody else would have known to make, and think, *How did he know they were going over there?*

It was good for me to have a solid group of players to teach me the ropes of playing defensive back in the NFL. But I also knew someone who helped teach me about glorifying God in all I do.

## Learning about the Master

I was blessed early in my relationship with Jesus Christ with men who had the courage to help teach me what the faith was all about. In Hartford, during that first summer I was saved, I had Astin Dakers. During my first year in Seattle, it was Dave Brown.

I first met Dave Brown in the summer of 1985, shortly after I moved to Seattle for training camp. When I first moved to Seattle, I began praying and fasting for the Seattle Seahawks—even though I wasn't yet on the team. I asked God to bless the Hawks, whether or not I made the team. I started attending church at Antioch Bible Church in Kirkland, which was pastored by former NFL player Ken Hutcherson, with Dave and his wife, Rhonda, and two boys, Aaron and Sterling. (Somewhere along the line, I became "Uncle Gene" to Aaron and Sterling. After I got married, I became their godfather.)

I still consider Dave Brown one of the biggest influences in my life. He helped me hone my walk with Jesus. I respected Dave greatly as a football player, and I still respect him as a man of God. In both areas, he was just solid in every way.

Dave Brown was an oustanding football player. He played on the Super Bowl X champion Pittsburgh Steelers team in 1975 before being picked up by the Seattle Seahawks in the expansion draft the following season. He was the last original Seahawk to play on the team. Dave Brown's and my careers paralleled one another in a lot of ways. He played eleven years in Seattle before going on to the Green Bay Packers, as did I. We also both have Super Bowl rings. Dave finished his fifteen years in the NFL with 62 interceptions, which tied him for sixth place all-time. He could—in my opinion *should*— end up in the Hall of Fame one day.

The most important thing Dave and I have in common is that we both love God. In retrospect, it seems like we were destined to become close friends. That's exactly what happened.

Dave took me under his wing during my rookie year in Seattle. He was my mentor on the football field and my discipler off it. He did that, I believe, because he saw in me a young man who was hungry for the Word of God. Dave had been walking with God for many years prior to that, and I think he wanted to impart to me the things he had learned and the wisdom he had acquired. The Word says in Proverbs 27:17: "As iron sharpens iron, so one man sharpens another." That's exactly what Dave Brown did for me.

Dave Brown taught me a lot about the NFL, about winning and losing, and about my relationship with God. I tried to emulate him in everything he did—on the field and off.

As my discipler, Dave did far more than just make sure I was at church on Sundays. Dave taught me how my profession as a player in the NFL could be used to glorify God. He changed my attitude about winning and about playing football. I still remember when he first talked to me about what it meant for the man of God to be a winner.

"Eugene, what do you think it means to be a winner?" he asked me.

"Well, you work hard and do your best to win the game, and you show good sportsmanship and walk across the field and shake a guy's hand," I said, basically regurgitating what I thought he wanted to hear.

"No!" he said. "It's none of that! It's to glorify God in *everything* you do. I want you to glorify God in everything you do. That's your goal."

Dave didn't say a word that day about winning football games or making good plays. All he talked about was glorifying God. That was revolutionary to me. I knew that I wanted to glorify God, but I had never thought about glorifying him when I played football.

Dave Brown knew the Word of God. That man knew what the Bible said, and he knew where it said it. He had memorized an incredible amount of Scripture, and he knew what it meant. He never let me get away with reciting a verse or a passage from the Bible without telling him where it was found.

"Where is that in the Bible?" Dave would ask when I recited something.

"I think it's in Old Testament," I'd answer.

"Well, that's in the right country."

If I had the right book, he'd say, "That's in the right state. Give me the city, the street address, and the house number."

Dave Brown didn't just challenge me to know the Word of God, but to apply it to live it out in every area of my daily life. He'd always tell me, "Don't just know it, Gene. Practice it." He could say that, too, because he didn't just know the Word of God but practiced it in every area of his life. He truly was an example of putting the Word into action.

Although I loved the man and respected him deeply, I would from time to time get aggravated at him when he challenged me. There were times when my pride got in the way of what God was trying to do in my life through Dave Brown, times when I wanted to rebel against his teaching. One of the times Dave Brown aggravated me was one day at practice during my first few years with the Seahawks. Chuck Knox had gotten after me about something. I had never felt like I was one of Coach Knox's favorite players, and that day I felt as if he was picking on me. I was working as hard as I could, but the best I got from him all day was a stare that said, "I don't appreciate your effort."

*What did I do this time?* I thought, as I stared back at him. I started back to the huddle, muttering, "Man, I'm tired of Chuck Knox. What do I have to do to please this guy?"

As I got to the huddle, my frustration spilled out in my speech. "Man, I can't believe it! Coach Knox won't leave me alone. What's his…"

Dave Brown looked at me and interrupted my rant: "The last time I checked, Philippians 2:14 says to do all things without complaining or murmuring, because it is God who works in you to do his will and his good pleasure."

Dave was right, and I knew it. But I didn't appreciate his reproof at that moment. I was too busy feeling frustrated and sorry for myself over what I perceived as an injustice that had been committed toward me.

"Man, do you just eat and breathe Bible stuff?" I shot back at him.

Dave didn't get angry or raise his voice. He just looked at me and asked me to explain that statement.

"What do you mean by that?" Dave asked me. "Do you mean, am I a Christian? am I a Christian who believes in the Word of God?"

I couldn't tell him what I meant. I knew he was right, and I knew I needed to ask God's forgiveness for my attitude. I said a short prayer right there on the field. I asked God to forgive me and to help me keep my attitude straight.

Dave Brown knew how to pray, and he helped me refine my prayer life. He taught me to be specific in what I prayed, to tell God exactly what I meant. I remember well how he corrected me one day when I made some mindless request of God as we prayed before a meal.

"Lord, I thank you for our food that we're about to receive. We ask that you use it to nourish our bodies and *feed our souls.*"

I had prayed that same thing a thousand times before, but that day Dave Brown looked at me and said, "It's impossible to feed your soul. The soul is the nonmaterial part of you that lives on forever—even after your body dies. How do you feed your soul with food?"

I said, "You know what I mean."

He said, "No I don't! What do you mean by 'feed your soul'? You said it, so tell me what you mean."

I told him he was right about that point, but, being the smart guy I was, I had a comeback for him: "Okay, you're right. You can't feed your soul with food. However, I prayed that this food will nourish my body so that I can do the work of God."

"Okay, then say that! When you pray, you need to say what you mean and mean what you say."

"Okay, Dave—say what I mean and mean what I say. I've got it."

Dave Brown and I went back and forth like that more times than I can remember. While he cut me no slack when it came to how I lived my Christian life, I loved being around him. I loved the fact that he loved God and cared enough about me to take the time to work with me.

Dave Brown helped me to learn about glorifying God in all that I do, but God used others on the team to teach me the lessons I needed to learn. One game, I learned a valuable—but tough—lesson about living out the Christian life in front of my teammates and my opponents.

## A Bitter Reproof

We were playing in the Kingdome—I don't remember who we were playing—and I was getting pretty cocky about how I was handling one of the players on our opponent's punt team. My job on the punt return team was to block the player who is called the "head hunter." I was beating this guy pretty badly—knocking him around the field. I handled him five straight times when I faced him. I was on the sidelines, telling my teammates, "Watch this! I'm beating this dude *down.*"

On the next play, I handled the same guy, and at the end of the play— *Bam!*—he punched me in the face. Right there in front of 65,000 fans, in front of my teammates, and in front of the officials. I was embarrassed. The first thing I did was appeal to the nearest official: "Hey, ref! Did you see that? That guy punched me right in the face!" But the official hadn't seen what happened. The player who had hit me in the face was smirking and laughing on his way off the field.

At that moment, I felt as if I was the victim of an injustice, and I was going to get some payback. I went back to the sideline, breathing fire and vowing vengeance. *Man, I'm gonna get that guy,* I thought. *I'm going to his head. We're going to throw down as soon as I get back on the field.*

I didn't think about the arrogance I had been demonstrating before I got punched. I didn't think about how my attitude was an offense to God and to his reputation. I didn't think about *my* sin. All I thought about was how I'd been offended, how my opponent had sinned against me.

Keith Simpson watched me storming up and down the sidelines and listened to the threats of revenge I was breathing on the sideline. Keith wasn't a believer, but God used him to put me in my place that afternoon.

"Man, when I get out there, I'm going to…"

"You're gonna do what, *Mr. Christian?*" Keith said, the sarcasm dripping from his words. "What are you gonna do? You know something? You're just like everybody else out here. You know it! You're no different."

Keith's words stung worse than any punch in the face. He was so right, and I was so wrong. I had forgotten who I was representing on the field. I had forgotten that my first priority on the field was to represent Jesus Christ in all that I do. I had forgotten who I was in Christ. I had forgotten that people who knew I was a Christian were watching me to see how I represented Jesus.

I looked so much like the rest of the world—the world of the NFL—that Keith Simpson couldn't see that I was different. At that moment, I wasn't. I truly was just like everybody else. I realized that I had sinned. I had offended God with my attitude and my actions.

I got off by myself on the sideline and asked for forgiveness: "Lord, I am just so sorry. I can't believe I'm doing this, and I can't believe the anger and hatred that is inside me. Lord, I just—"

"PUNT RETURN TEAM!"

It was time for me to get out there. *Not now! I don't want to get into a fight with this guy! I don't want to misrepresent you out here on this football field. Lord, help me to glorify you in what happens now.*

I lined up on the same guy who had punched me the play before. This time, I didn't want to touch him. I didn't want to cause further strife. I didn't want to demonstrate the kind of pride and arrogance I had been carrying around on the field that day. I just wanted to do my job in a manner pleasing to God.

At the snap of the ball, he ran down the field, and I ran just fast enough to stay in front of him. I just wanted to get in his way and not do anything that would escalate the situation. After our punt returner was tackled, I looked up, and the guy who had punched me was walking toward me. *Oh no! I don't want to fight this guy!* I started to back up as he walked toward me, but he walked up to me and put his arm on my shoulder and said, "I'm sorry for punching you. Can you forgive me?"

I don't know if the guy was a believer. I just knew how relieved I felt that he didn't want to fight. I screamed at the top of my lungs, "Yeah! I forgive you! I totally forgive you!"

I had learned a valuable lesson that day, a lesson that has never left me. That day I realized that as a Christian man playing a violent game, I'm being watched by those who know I love Jesus. I'm being watched by men who want to know if I truly am different.

It was a tough lesson, but a lesson I needed to learn.

## Learning Confidence in a Roller-Coaster Season

A lot of people thought the Seahawks were going to be a major factor in the American Football Conference in 1985. The team was coming off a 12–4 play-off season and looking forward to the return of running back Curt

Warner, who had missed most of 1984 with a knee injury. Seattle also had one of the best defenses in the NFL, and quarterback Dave Krieg had one of the best seasons passing in the history of the league in 1984.

Expectations can be hard to live up to, and the Seahawks didn't come close to living up to them in 1985, finishing with the strangest 8–8 record in the history of the league. We won our first two games, then finished the season on a lose-lose/win-win pattern. That's right, we never won more than two games in a row, and we never lost more than two straight.

In 1984 the Seahawks had won with a bend-but-don't-break defense that got timely interceptions, fumble recoveries, and blocked kicks. In the roller coaster that was the 1985 season, we didn't get those big plays. For some reason, we just couldn't create breaks for ourselves.

While the Seahawks fans started to grow disenchanted with the team and with Coach Knox's style, I finished out the year getting a big shot of confidence. I'd played very sparingly on our regular defense for most of the season, but during the last two games of the year I played extensively at strong safety because of injuries to Ken Easley and Paul Moyer. I led the team in tackles those two games—against the Los Angeles Raiders and Denver—including a season high 9 tackles against the Broncos in our finale.

My confidence was going through the roof. I knew I could play in the NFL. I knew I belonged here. It was time for me to seize the opportunity to build on what I had done late in the season.

I was looking forward to getting started on the 1986 season. I couldn't wait to go out and enjoy the blessings that God had given me on the football field. I knew it was going to be a big season.

And it would also be a season I would share intimately with a very important person in my life.

## CHAPTER SEVEN

# COMMITTING MYSELF TO GIA

I n my study I have numerous reminders of the success I've enjoyed as a
player in the National Football League. I have several game balls I've
received after making big plays to help my team win important games. I
have trophies, awards, and photographs commemorating things I've done in
the league.

All of these are mementos to a career that has truly seen the blessing of
God. They are reminders to me that he has guided my career and given me
success.

While I enjoy the success I've had and the recognition I've received since
I first came into the league in 1985, I have to tell you that those things
wouldn't mean a thing to me if not for two things: my relationship with God
and my family.

Success is hollow if you don't have someone to share it with, and God
has blessed me with a beautiful, loving wife and two great kids to help me
enjoy the blessings he's given me as a professional athlete.

God sent me the first part of that blessing—Gia—before my rookie season in Seattle ended.

## A Lonely Time

My rookie year in the National Football League was a learning time for me, a
time when I grew as a football player, as a person, and as a man of God. It
was a time when I made lasting friendships with men who influenced me
more than anyone I'd ever met—or have met since. But it was also a time

when I felt a huge void in my life. It was a time when I missed Gia. I wanted to be with her—permanently.

After I got saved, my relationship with Gia—after a short hiatus while I got myself grounded in the faith—grew. Immediately after I got saved, Gia took the backseat in my life. I spent all my time with Astin Dakers. I never stopped caring about Gia, but Jesus had my undivided attention. Soon, it was time for me to return to Colgate.

Somehow, God kept Gia and me together. We continued our relationship through my senior year. Even though we didn't attend the same college, we made time for one another. The more time I spent with her, the more I realized I wanted to make this beautiful, graceful, godly woman my wife. We got engaged in June of 1985—shortly before I went to Seattle to try out with the Seahawks. We planned to get married the following June, after Gia's college graduation.

Proverbs 16:9 says, "In his heart a man plans his course, but the LORD determines his steps." When I asked Gia to marry me, I had every intention of finishing my first year with the Seahawks before we got married. Likewise, Gia wanted to finish her college education. But God had a different plan.

## Let's Do It!

I was miserable being away from Gia—me living and working in Seattle and her living in Connecticut, where she was attending Hartford University. I talked to her on the phone as much as possible, but it wasn't the same as being with her.

That August, we decided we weren't going to wait. After I had made the Seahawks' roster, I called her and said, "I don't want to wait any longer. Let's get married as soon as we can."

The way I saw it, if it's right, it's right, and there's no reason to put it off. I didn't want to wait, and neither did Gia. I prayed about the situation and asked God to give me direction. It wasn't long before I knew what to do.

Gia and I decided to get married on October 1. That was on a Tuesday, my day off. While I was in Seattle, Gia took care of all the arrangements. She invited our friends and family and arranged for us to be wed at her church in Hartford.

I had a game with the Seahawks that Sunday at Kansas City. Although I had a huge day coming that Tuesday (my wedding day), I kept my mind focused on what was before me. It was tough, though. I couldn't wait to be with Gia.

Our wedding day was quite a departure from the norm. Most guys in the NFL would have waited until the season was over to get married. That way, they'd have time for their honeymoons, and they wouldn't be rushed. I couldn't do that, though. I wanted to get this finished.

I flew back to Hartford on Tuesday, where Gia and I were married in front of more than a hundred friends and family members. We had a receiving line for our guests, then at 8:30 got back on a plane for Seattle. We got home about midnight, and I was back to work the following morning, getting ready for our upcoming game.

Our wedding was an exciting, memorable time for both Gia and me. And it marked the beginning of a relationship that God has blessed immensely. With our wedding behind us, it was time for us to get on to the business of living as husband and wife.

## Enduring Marriage

I always tell people that being a Christian isn't easy. As a Christian, your life is in direct opposition to the ways of this world. You're standing for things that are often unpopular in the eyes of a sinful, fallen human race.

Being married is like that in a lot of ways. It's not always easy, because marriage is an arrangement where two fallen, selfish people are put together in a situation where they have to live together. Marriage is a union where two people who want their own way are forced to yield to each other's needs and desires.

Like the Christian life, marriage isn't easy, but it can be done. It takes a lot of love, commitment, self-sacrifice, and faith—and it takes endurance. Also like the Christian life, when you do it the way God says to do it, the rewards are incredible.

Nobody teaches you how to live the married life. Sure, there are tons of books and seminars out there—both Christian and secular—but there are really no ironclad guarantees when you get married. The only blueprint you have is from God—in his written Word, the Bible.

## Eugene, Love Your Wife...

When God spoke through the apostle Paul in Ephesians 5:25, he told us husbands what it takes to make our marriages successful: "Husbands, love your wives, just as Christ loved the church and gave himself up for her."

I've heard people ask why God tells us to do something so obvious as love our wives. I believe it's because loving our wives isn't something that we, in our fleshly states, do naturally. Sorry guys, but we don't naturally love the way women do. Women, it seems, more naturally do the things entailed in loving. For example, if you ask a woman how she feels, she'll tell you right now. If you ask a man the same thing, he'll stammer and stutter, then give some stock answer like, "Fine! How about you?"

God knows that about us men, so he tells us to love our wives the same way Jesus loves us: sacrificially. He's given us a goal in our marriages, and that is to sacrifice ourselves for our wives, to love them through our words and actions. That's tough for us men, because in our fallen natures we're selfish. I can see that in my own life. Day in and day out I prove that I'm selfish. I need to be reminded that my job as Gia's husband is to lay aside my selfishness and sacrifice myself for her and nurture her.

While Gia may understand how to do that for me, I don't always know how to do it for her. Sometimes Gia has to tell me what she needs. She may assume that I know what to do to meet her needs. I've had to tell her, "Gia, I don't know what you need. What are you asking? What are you saying? Honey, I'm not trying to be a knucklehead. I just don't always understand what you need unless you tell me."

Sometimes the things Gia wants from me are things I never would have thought were that important to her. For example, she may want me to call her and tell her I was thinking about her when we're apart. She might want me to do some small thing that tells her how much I love her. She knows that I love her, but she wants to hear me say it or demonstrate it in some small way.

I feel greatly blessed because Gia has done a great job of helping me understand the little differences between men and women—those difference that, if handled lovingly, can make a marriage great but can also tear two people apart when handled carelessly.

## She's the One!

When people meet Gia, they see a beautiful, graceful woman with a radiant smile and a warm, loving personality. There's no question that Gia is physically beautiful. I remember being smitten the first time I saw her, thinking *That's the woman I'm going to marry!* But I've come to find out that there's a lot more to her than her looks.

Gia is a woman of incredible intelligence, wisdom, and wit. And she loves God with all her heart. She has a vibrant, growing relationship with the Lord, and she knows the Word. She is an obedient servant of Jesus Christ, and she is submitted to doing his will in every area of her life.

I've had a lot of fun being married to Gia. Not only is she beautiful and sweet, she's also one of the funniest people I've ever known. She's got a great sense of humor, and she knows how to make me laugh. I'm a guy who enjoys a good joke (just ask any of my teammates), and Gia's a great audience. Sometimes she and I get to laughing when we're together.

While Gia loves to laugh and make me laugh, she is very serious about obeying the Word of God. She is obedient to Paul's words in Colossians 3:18: "Wives, submit to your husbands, as is fitting in the Lord." She may not always feel like doing that, but she does it, knowing that God will use her submission to her husband to bless us in our marriage and in our parenthood.

It's not always easy for a woman to submit to her husband. That's why Paul makes a point of saying to do so. *Submission* is not a popular word today. It means putting yourself under somebody else's authority, and in our fleshly, fallen states, we don't want to do that.

Gia knows that she can submit herself to my authority because she knows that I want to be obedient to the Word of God myself. Yes, I blow it, and Gia would be the first to tell you that I don't always do things right. But Gia knows that my heart is with doing what God tells me to do when it comes to our family. Gia also knows that I understand that submission doesn't mean that she becomes a robot and blindly obeys my every word. In fact, she knows that it means that I'm also submitted and obedient to her. My wife is one of my most important counselors. If I've got a decision to make, I go to this wise woman and talk to her about it. For example, if someone offers me a financial opportunity, I will always go to Gia and ask her first: "Gia, what do you think?" If she says, "I don't feel right about it" there's no question what I am to do next. "Sorry, I can't do it! My wife and I can't agree on it, and it isn't worth strife in my marriage."

I'm not embarrassed to tell you that my wife has saved us a lot of money by keeping me from making bad decisions. She's the one who makes most of those decisions in the Robinson household because, frankly, I'm terrible at those things. (It also helps that Gia and I don't look at the money that comes into our home as "my money," or "her money," or even "our money." It's God's money, and it's his to do with as he sees fit. We're just the stewards.)

Gia and I don't always agree on everything that comes up. Sometimes I want to do something that she isn't sure about. We've argued before, and we've even gotten angry at one another. I always say that if a married couple doesn't argue, then they don't communicate. If you live with another human being, you're going to have arguments. But I've learned that tears are okay and arguments are fine— as long as we work out those things in the framework of a godly marriage. We live by the scriptural admonition in Ephesians 4:26 that says, "In your anger do not sin. Do not let the sun go down while you are still angry."

Gia and I are committed to loving one another, respecting one another, and submitting to one another. That's what God has told us to do, and we obey. The blessings that come because of our obedience are incredible.

And two of those blessings are the best of all.

## Leaving a Legacy

I am overwhelmed at times when I think about the blessings God has given Gia and me. We have a great marriage, a nice home, lots of good friends. But all those things pale in comparison with the two greatest blessings of all: Brittany and Brandon.

God blessed us with a daughter and a son who are healthy, happy, intelligent, and athletic. They're just great kids in every way. And they're kids who will grow up knowing the importance of a strong relationship with the Lord.

Children aren't just a great blessing from God; they're also a tremendous responsibility. You have to provide everything for them—their physical needs, their emotional needs, and their spiritual needs. As parents who love God, Gia and I are responsible for leaving our children a legacy of knowing Jesus Christ. We know that we're going to make mistakes as we endeavor to instill that in our kids, but we want to maintain a consistent walk before them as an example of what godly people look like.

We want our children to grow up knowing what they are to be like as children of God. We want them to know who they are in Christ and how they can give to the kingdom of God. We want them to treat people with kindness and compassion. We want them to be able to tell others about their faith. I don't care if my kids become doctors, lawyers, or professional athletes—I just want them to have those qualities.

My wife and I have prayed for those things in our children since we found out she was pregnant with Brittany, and we have continued to pray for those things ever since.

I prayed for Brittany before she was born. I used to bend down by my wife's stomach and pray for her and read Psalms and Proverbs to her. I prayed that she would grow up to love God and his Word. I remember praying for Brandon when he was an infant. I picked him up out of his swing when he was three months old and I held him up to God and prayed for him. I prayed for his spouse. I prayed that he would be a mighty man of God, that he would love God with all his heart and soul and strength, that he would grow up in the fear and admonition of the Lord. I prayed that God would use him, no matter what line of work he went into.

Gia and I have spent countless hours in prayer for our children—together and apart. But there's more to raising kids to love God and others than prayer. It also takes teaching—both in the words that we say and in our actions.

## Teaching Them the Way

The Word says in Proverbs 22:6, "Train a child in the way he should go, and when he is old he will not turn from it." Praying for your children is important, but that prayer has to be accompanied by godly teaching.

Gia and I teach our kids about what it means to be godly. We teach them about prayer, about reading the Bible, about showing other people kindness and compassion, and about living the kind of life God calls them to live.

When we teach them about prayer, we tell them that if they have a problem, pray about it. We tell them to let God know how much they appreciate all that he does for them. We tell them to pray for other people, even those who might be giving them a hard time or who aren't their close friends. We also teach them how important it is for them to read God's Word and apply it to their lives.

Gia and I try to teach our children the importance of the words, "I'm sorry. Will you forgive me?" We teach them that those words are important because they aren't going to make the right decisions all the time.

Not long ago, I had the opportunity to see that take hold of my daughter as she learned the importance of kindness to one of her classmates at school.

Ten-year-old girls tend to be very cliquish, and they'll ostracize girls who don't "fit in." That happened to one little girl in my daughter's school, and Brittany got caught up in that. One day I talked to her about it.

"Let me ask you this, Brittany: You're a popular girl, but how would you feel if you were the girl who wasn't popular?" I asked. "What do think goes through her mind when no one will talk to her or play with her?"

"I'd feel real bad, Daddy," she said. "I need to apologize to her and make sure that doesn't happen again."

A few days later, Brittany told me, "Hey Dad, I went to that girl and I talked to her. I told her I don't want her to feel left out or like no one cares about her."

I said, "Britt, you're doing some good stuff."

I was proud of Brittany for understanding the importance of going to someone and apologizing and asking for forgiveness when she blows it.

Brittany has had a chance to learn that from her dad, who makes his share of mistakes. She had a chance to see it up close and personal one chilly, snowy morning in Green Bay.

## Forgive Me?

We were going through the chaos of getting the kids ready for school—getting breakfast served, homework prepared, and lunches made. Brandon was out the door and waiting for the bus while Brittany was still inside, taking care of a few last-minute details before she left for the day. Just then, the bus stopped in front of the house, and Brandon got on.

Brittany wanted to go out and get on the bus, but now she couldn't. She was embarrassed. She didn't want to walk out late, in front of everybody, and in a hurry to catch the bus. She didn't want the other kids to laugh at her for making the bus wait for her, even for a few seconds. That might not sound like a big problem for an adult, but it's huge for a ten-year-old girl. I didn't understand it.

"Let's go, Britt!" I said. "You gotta catch the bus!"

"Daddy, I can't go out there now!" she protested. "The other kids will laugh at me!"

"I don't care about that! Dad wants you on the bus! Let's go!"

She was embarrassed, and she was trying to tell me about it. But I didn't hear her. I wasn't even trying to hear her. All I knew (again, here's the goal-oriented part of me coming out) was that she needed to go to school and that the bus would take her to school, so she needed to get on the bus to get there.

The bus left and went around the block, then stopped to pick her up. Now it was worse. Not only did the bus have to wait for her, now it had to make a special stop just to pick her up.

"Dad, I can't do that!" Brittany cried.

"Get out there and get on the bus, Britt! What is the big deal?"

Finally, she left and got on the bus and went to school. I, on the other hand, knew I had blown it with my daughter. I felt rotten. I couldn't stop thinking about how I had hurt my little girl's feelings, how I had belittled her emotions like that. I love my kids, and there's nothing I wouldn't do to protect them from being hurt. Now I was the cause of my daughter's emotional pain. My heart was about to burst. I had to make amends.

I jumped in my car, drove down to the school, and went to the office. The people at the office started a conversation with me about the Packers. I talked to them a little, then got to the point of my visit. "Actually, I'm here to see my daughter. Could you bring her out for me?" They called her down to the office and I took her outside to talk.

"Brittany, you know what?" I said. "Daddy was mean and grumpy this morning. I forgot what it was like to be ten or eleven years old. You said you didn't want to go on the bus and have the kids laugh at you, but I didn't listen. I know that's a big deal. I'm sorry. Will you forgive me?"

"Oh, Daddy," she cried, "I'm sorry too! Don't worry about it."

"No, honey. I have to apologize to you. I will never make you feel guilty about being embarrassed about something. I won't make you do something that you feel embarrassed doing. I'll have much more compassion for you next time. I need your forgiveness. Will you forgive Dad?"

My daughter never kissed me in public. She'll hug me, sometimes, but never kiss me. This time, she put her arms around me and kissed me, right there in front of the school. "Yeah, Daddy!" she said. "I forgive you. I love you, Dad!"

"Thank you, honey." I said. "Let's go by Brandon's room and wave to him."

Brittany and I walked upstairs to say hi to Brandon. I walked to the door of his classroom, and one of his buddies said to him, "Hey Brandon, your dad's here." Brandon looked at me, and I flashed him a hand signal that means "I love you." He flashed it back at me. I walked Brittany back to her room, gave her a hug, then headed to practice.

## Doing Unto Others...

Gia and I always try to teach our kids the value of treating others with respect and kindness, and the lessons more often than not begin at home. My son had a chance to learn about that at one of Brittany's recent school events.

Both of our kids are athletic. Brittany runs track—she does sprints, relays, and the long jump—and does gymnastics, and Brandon plays football. Recently, during the NFL's off-season, Brandon and I went to one of Brittany's track meets in Woodinville, Washington, our hometown. It was a typical spring day in the Seattle area: cool and rainy. We were dressed for the weather, but Brandon wasn't particularly enjoying the rain.

"Daddy, let's go to the car," Brandon said, just as Brittany was about to run an event.

"We can't go to the car now," I said. "Brittany's running now!"

"When is Brittany finished?"

"Pretty soon. Then we can go get in the car."

"Where's Mom?"

"Mom's not here yet. She'll be here later."

Finally, I realized I had to use this moment to teach my son something. I reminded him of when he played flag football in Green Bay and how Brittany had stayed out in the cold weather to watch him play.

"Remember when we were at your football game that day and you threw the winning pass and you scored the two points?" I reminded him. "It was cold out there that day, wasn't it?"

"Yeah, it was."

"Who was there?"

"You, Mom, and Brittany," he said, the point of my questioning obviously starting to take hold of him.

"Well, it was fun having Brittany there, wasn't it?"

"Yeah."

"Well, guess what?" I said. "It's raining and cold out here today, and we're going to stay and watch Brittany do her thing."

To me, this was another example of the kinds of things God wants me to do as a father. It was another opportunity for me and my kids to learn to be more like him.

## Reaping the Rewards

I can't think of many things that are more rewarding than to make God and his Word the center of your marriage and family. When Gia and I came into our marriage, we had both committed our lives to the Lord Jesus Christ. And because we were living for him, he made our marriage and our role as parents everything that it could and should be.

And because of that, my ministry and my profession in the National Football League took on new importance.

## ESTABLISHING MYSELF IN THE NFL

# EARNING PLAYING TIME

I was on top of the world heading into the 1986 National Football League season. I'd gotten married the previous October, I'd closed out the 1985 season strongly, and I knew I had a chance to be a key player on the '86 Seahawks. I've always been a confident football player. I've never been intimidated by much of anything. But coming into my second year with Seattle, I thought there was nothing I couldn't do on the football field, no test I couldn't endure.

I came into camp ready to make a major contribution to the Seattle Seahawks. Even though I wasn't sure what the coaches had in mind for me, I knew I was capable of playing on the regular defense on a full-time basis.

I had played strong safety at the end of my rookie year, filling in for Ken Easley when he was injured. I got another break at the beginning of the 1986 season. John Harris, Seattle's starting free safety, held out of training camp because of a contract dispute. I was the Hawks' insurance policy, their ace in the hole. The coaches knew I could play, and that put them in a good position to bargain with Harris. In the end, though, they traded him to the Minnesota Vikings. I had the opportunity I had hoped for. It was time for me to seize the moment.

With John Harris gone, the free safety spot was open, with myself and Paul Moyer vying for the position. I had a great training camp. I had 3 interceptions in the preseason games and was among the team leaders in tackles. I made some great hits, too. As we football players like to say, I was putting some wood on folks. My play caught the Seahawk coaches' attention, and I wound up starting all sixteen games that season at free safety.

My first season as a starter was a good one for me. I was second on the team in tackles and led the Seahawks in fumble recoveries. I felt good about the way I'd played in 1986, but it was a disappointing season for the Seahawks. We finished a respectable 10–6, but we missed making the play-offs. We showed how good we could be in beating the American Football Conference champion Denver Broncos 41–16 in the final week of the season and handing the Super Bowl XXI champion New York Giants one of their two losses that season, 17–12 at the Kingdome. But we also showed how bad we could be, losing four in a row at one point, including a horrible three-game stretch where we were outscored 99–21.

The great news for us was that we finished as one of the hottest teams in the league, winning our final five games to move into contention for the play-offs. We were considered one of the teams to beat in the AFC in 1987. We had a strong defense—led by Ken Easley, who would be healthy for the first time in two seasons when the season began—a hot quarterback in Dave Krieg, a great set of running backs in Curt Warner and John L. Williams, and a receiving corps led by the great Steve Largent.

On paper, we were a team to be feared. On the field, however, we were a disappointment, finishing 9–6 and slipping into the play-offs as a wild-card team, where we lost 23–20 in overtime to the Houston Oilers. It was a disappointing end to a mediocre season, a season in which we expected much more of ourselves.

The 1987 season was a tough one for everybody in the league—the players, the coaches, the management, and the ownership. It was a year that taught everybody something about endurance. It was the year of the players' strike, the second work stoppage of the decade for the league. The teams all played their first two games of the season before the strike began. The third week of the season saw all its games canceled, and that was followed by three weeks of games played by "replacement players." While the players walked picket lines, the league continued operations—using as players men who only a few weeks before had no chance of playing professional football.

It was a time everybody was glad to put behind them, a time when the league was open to public ridicule. When the season was finished, everybody—players, coaches, management, fans—looked forward to a new start in 1988.

## Mired in Mediocrity

The Seahawks won the AFC Western Division championship in 1988, but we didn't have a great season. We finished first at 9–7 in what everybody knew was a down year for the division. With two games left in the season, we were 7–7. We beat Denver 42–14 at the Kingdome and the Los Angeles Raiders 43–37 at the L. A. Coliseum to win the division.

Although I was awarded a game ball after the game with the Raiders, there wasn't a lot of defense being played that day. The two teams combined for 931 yards of total offense, including Dave Krieg's 410 yards passing. We secured the win on the Raiders' last possession when Nesby Glasgow knocked down Jay Schroeder's pass to the back of the end zone.

We got bumped in our first play-off game, 21–13 by the Cincinnati Bengals at Riverfront Stadium.

When I look at the year I had in 1988, it was kind of a mixed bag. I led the team in tackles with a career-high 115 stops to become the first Seattle Seahawk defensive back to lead the team in stops since Dave Brown in 1976. While that might sound like a great season, it's not good when a free safety leads his team in tackles. That means the opposition's running backs are getting loose in the defensive backfield. That's what was happening with us. We were among the worst teams in the league at stopping the run that season. Teams were just teeing off on us up front. We played a 3–4 defense—three down linemen and four linebackers—and that, I believe, gave teams more of an opportunity to run on us.

I've always preferred a 4–3 defense, and the 1988 season was a great example of why. I like to have four big guys up front creating havoc with the offense's line. I like to see them shooting the gaps, disrupting the offense's blocking schemes, and freeing up the linebackers to make tackles. When you have only three defensive linemen, that leaves four linebackers out there battling with offensive linemen who most of the time are a lot bigger and stronger than they are.

## Growing as a Player

I was coming into my own as a player during those early years with the Seattle Seahawks. I was growing bigger and stronger—remember, I came into the league weighing about 180 pounds—and I was getting better all the time at the physical aspect of the game. I was learning how to play my position. I was a good hitter when I came into the league, but I learned how to play the ball more and not look as much for the big hits. Those still came, but so did my consistency as a football player. I was getting better and better all the time at playing the pass and at taking care of my responsibilities. When I first came into the league, I wanted to do everything, but I found out I was of much more value to my team when I played my own position and took care of my own responsibilities.

Those lessons became more and more important as I progressed in my career—and as the Seattle Seahawks *regressed* as a team.

## Sinking below Mediocrity

The 1988 National Football League season was to be Seattle's last as a play-off participant for quite some time. In fact, as of the 1997 campaign the Seahawks still hadn't made it to the postseason. The team began to lose players to retirement, injury, and free agency, and a string of poor drafts had left us without the kind of players it takes to contend for the play-offs. Key starters such as center Blair Bush and tight end Mike Tice left Seattle to sign with other teams. In addition, players like Steve Largent, Jacob Green, Curt Warner, and Joe Nash, while still quality players, were past their prime.

In 1989, I endured my first losing season in professional football as the Seahawks finished 7–9. We had a shot at a nonlosing (.500) season heading into the final game of the year, but a 29–0 blowout to the Washington

Redskins doomed us to a losing record.

There wasn't much reason for anybody to expect things to get better for us in 1990. Steve Largent retired at the age of thrity-five and Curt Warner signed with the Los Angeles Rams. Mike Wilson, a starting tackle for the Seahawks since his arrival in 1986, also retired. Somehow, though, we had a decent season in 1990, finishing 9–7 and missing the play-offs for the second year in a row. We won some close games, including back-to-back 13–10 overtime wins over San Diego and Houston in weeks eleven and twelve, and we lost some close ones, including a 34–31 overtime loss to the Denver Broncos at Mile High Stadium in week three.

We enjoyed the winning record, but it would be our last in Seattle. From then on, it was all downhill. After another 7–9 season in 1991, the Seattle Seahawks embarked on their worst season ever.

## Enduring a Tough Season

Mark Twain once said something about there being three kinds of lies, the third kind being statistics. Anybody with any familiarity at all with professional football knows you can't always trust statistics. They might be a fun diversion for the fans, but they don't always tell the whole story.

Of course, there are times when statistics give you as honest a picture of a team as anything. The 1992 Seattle Seahawks were an example of that.

We finished 2–14 that season. The reason? We couldn't score any points. In fact, we couldn't even move the ball. We set records for offensive futility that season, including the one that counts the most: points scored. We scored a league-record low (in a sixteen-game schedule) 140 points. That's an average of *less than* 10 points per game. We were shut out twice and scored only 3 points three times. We never scored more than 17 points in a game. We finished last in the league in total offense, passing offense, and scoring. We finished in the bottom third of the league in rushing offense, turnovers, and sacks allowed.

Actually, a tough season for the Seahawks in 1992 wasn't unexpected. Dave Krieg, who had quarterbacked the team since 1983, had left and signed with Kansas City. Chuck Knox had left to coach the Los Angeles Rams, leaving the team in the hands of Tom Flores. The team also had suffered through an injury-filled season on the offensive line and elsewhere. That season the Seahawks set a team record by having twenty-two players on injured reserve. Those players missed a combined total of 180 games.

I don't want to sound critical of the players who were on the Seattle offensive team that season. They played hard all season and they never quit, even when we were hopelessly behind in games. They were men I respected and loved as people. But the combination of a lack of experience at quarterback, on the offensive line, and at receiver doomed the team to a poor year on offense.

We played several games in 1992 where we kept the score close enough to have a chance to win. The reason? We had one of the best defenses in the National Football League. Statistically, we finished in the top ten in the league in total defense, which is incedible when you consider the amount of time the defense was on the field because of our lack of offense.

The heart and soul of our defense was defensive tackle Cortez Kennedy, who came to the Seahawks in 1990 as the team's first-round draft pick. At six-feet-three-inches tall and 295 pounds, 'Tez was—and still is—dominant. It literally took three men to block the guy. He just had his way on the field. He was dominant against the run and in the pass rush. Because he played on a bad team, Cortez Kennedy was a pretty well-kept secret from fans of the NFL. Not from the players and coaches, though. They knew what he could do because many of them tried to stop him from doing it. They respected him so much that he was named the NFL Defensive Player of the Year in 1992—an astonishing honor when you consider he played for a team that won two games all season.

We had solid linebackers, too, in outside men Terry Wooden and Rufus Porter, and middle linebacker Dave Wyman. Add to that a defensive backfield of Patrick Hunter and Dwayne Harper at cornerback, Robert Blackmon at strong safety and myself at free safety, and you have a solid defense.

The 1992 Seahawks defense was full of character guys, guys who refused to quit, no matter how tough things got. We really learned how to stick together. It surprises some people to hear me say this, but the teams we played against respected our defense. We were 2–14, but after games, guys would tell me, "You guys ain't no joke. You can play!"

I had a great year in 1992, finishing first on the team with 94 tackles in addition to tying for the American Football Conference lead in interceptions with 7. (I tied Ken Easley's record of 3 interceptions in a game when I got three picks in our 20–14 loss to the Steelers in Pittsburgh.) I was honored that season with my first trip to the Pro Bowl. In addition, I was named second-team All-AFC by *College & Pro Football Newsweekly.*

The 1992 season was a memorable one for me, not because of wins and losses on the football field, but because of what it taught me about endurance. When I think of the word *endurance* I think of my teammates on the Seattle Seahawk defense that season. They were guys who knew the value of never giving up, even in what seemed like the most hopeless of situations. Our endurance and perseverance may not have translated into more wins for our team, but I saw in that group men who knew the importance of sticking together in adverse situations and of not giving up.

To me, that looked like an excellent foundation from which to build a solid football team.

## Nowhere to Go but Up

After a tough year in 1992, people around the Seattle Seahawks organization—the players, the coaches, and the fans—felt the team could only get better in 1993. We still had a formidable defense and our offense had to improve, with the additions of rookie quarterback Rick Mirer and free agents Kelvin Martin and Ferrell Edmunds.

The Seahawks got Mirer after a coin flip with the New England Patriots, who also won only two games in 1992, to determine the first and second picks in the draft. The Patriots won the coin toss and selected Drew Bledsoe from Washington State. We got Rick Mirer, who played college ball at Notre Dame, with the second pick of the draft.

Rick Mirer came into the league with a splash. As a starter his first game out, Rick was able to provide instant improvement to the Seattle offense. No, we weren't going to challenge the San Francisco 49ers' supremacy in offensive football, but there was noticeable improvement almost from the start. In addition to giving us a passing threat, Rick helped keep opposing defenses from stacking up against the run, and we were able to lead the AFC in rushing (we were ninth out of fourteen teams in 1992).

We started the season with consecutive losses to the San Diego Chargers and the Los Angeles Raiders—by a total of 10 points—then did what most people thought was unthinkable: we went on a three-game winning streak to go 3–2 after five games. We were 4–3 after seven games, but finished out by losing seven of our last nine games to finish 6–10. Not exactly an eye-popping record, but well on the way to respectability.

I was blessed with another great year in 1993, a year in which I was again named to the Pro Bowl as a reserve safety. I finished with 9 interceptions to tie with Buffalo's Nate Odomes for the NFL lead. I was also named All-NFL by several publications and second-team All-NFL by the Associated Press.

There was a feeling among the Seattle Seahawks that we would continue to improve during the following season. We did, too, but by the end of the season I wasn't around to enjoy it.

## An Abbreviated Season

After two straight trips to the Pro Bowl and after being voted the captain of the defense by my teammates, I was looked at as the leader of the Seattle Seahawk defense heading into the 1994 season. It was a great blessing to me to have my teammates look to me for leadership like that, and it also afforded me a great opportunity to minister to many of my teammates.

I looked forward to seeing what the team could accomplish on the field in 1994, and we started out strong, winning three of our first four. After that though, we took a step backwards, losing five in a row to fall to 3–6. We played .500 football the rest of the way, getting our last win of the season in a game that I remember well. It was a game where for the first time in my professional football career, I suffered an injury that required me to miss games.

We were playing the Houston Oilers in the Astrodome on December 12, when for no reason that I could tell, my right Achilles tendon popped. I was backpedaling the same way I'd done thousands of times during my high school, college, and professional football careers when it happened. I was about to break for the ball when it felt like somebody hit me in the back of my ankle with a stick. It also made a vibrating sound when it happened. At first I thought I'd collided with an official. I turned around to say, "Hey man, you've got to get out of the way when I'm backpedaling," but there was no one around me. By this time I was on the ground, trying to get up.

I thought I was all right, but as I looked up I saw the Seahawks' team doctor coming toward me shaking his head. He knew what it was before he got to me. "It looks like you've popped your Achilles," he said. It didn't hurt badly at all, and I thought I was going to be okay. I said, "I can run though, Doc!" then tried to get up.

The doctor just looked at me and shook his head. "You can't do anything," he said.

The next day I had surgery to repair my Achilles tendon. After that, it was time for that painful process called rehab. Fortunately, my body heals remarkably quickly. It always has. That ability to heal quickly proved to be a blessing for me as I embarked on my eleventh season with Seattle.

## A New Start

The Seattle Seahawks started a new era in 1995—the Dennis Erickson era. Tom Flores was dismissed from his coaching duties following the 1994 campaign, and owner Ken Behring brought in a local product to take his place. Erickson, who had been the head football coach at the University of Miami before coming to the Seahawks, grew up in the Seattle area and had coached at Washington State University before moving on to coach the Hurricanes.

There's no question the Seattle Seahawks would have a different look in 1995. For me, the question was whether I would be rehabilitated enough before the season started to play at full strength.

I did some rehab exercises during that off-season, and by the time our first minicamp rolled around the following spring, I was ready to go. I was running full speed during the first minicamp. In my second minicamp, which was held in May, I still felt no ill effects from the injury, but when training camp started, my ankle began to get stiff and sore. I could run, but it hurt. I felt like I'd taken a step backwards in getting back to where I'd been before, but the doctor told me that it took about eight months to be completely recovered. I continued to practice in training camp and prepare for the 1995 season, and when the season started, I wasn't as effective in the early part of the season as I had been before the injury. I wasn't getting abused or anything like that, but I wasn't making the kind of plays I was used to making. But I endured the pain, and, slowly but surely, it subsided, and by the middle of October—during a bye week—the pain was gone.

From then on, I just took off. I finished the season with just 1 interception, but I recorded 105 tackles—all while not missing a snap all season.

I started out the 1995 season slowly but improved as the season went on and finished strongly. The same was true of the Seahawks as a team. We started out miserably, losing six of our first eight games before rebounding to finish 8–8. It looked like we were on the verge of bigger and better things.

## Where Will I (We) Be?

All the major football publications said that the Seattle Seahawks were one of the most improved teams in the National Football League. As the cliché goes, we were "a team on the rise." After suffering through a 2–14 season in 1992, Seahawks fans got a limited taste of success in 1995. They wanted more, and there was a new sense of enthusiasm in the Emerald City for its football team.

Tampering the enthusiasm, though, was the uncertainty over whether the Seahawks would stay in Seattle. Seahawks owner Ken Behring attempted to move the team, which had been in Seattle since 1976, to Los Angeles. The National Football League stepped in and stopped Behring from holding the team's practices in Anaheim, and Washington's King County, where Seattle is located, sued to force him to honor the team's contract and stay in Seattle. In the end, the Seahawks stayed put—at least for the '96 season.

Now the question for me was, would *I* be staying in Seattle?

## ◄ MOVING ON ►

# JOINING A CONTENDER IN GREEN BAY

There's something about uncertainty that really shows you where you're at in your relationship with God. When you don't know what your future holds, you have two choices: lean on God and on his plan for you, or drive yourself crazy with worry.

That's the situation I was faced with following the 1995 National Football League season, my eleventh with Seattle. Not only was the future of the team itself uncertain, it started to look more and more during the off-season that I may not have a spot on the team in 1996.

I'd already accomplished far more in the league than anyone had any reason to expect when I arrived in Seattle fresh out of my senior year at Colgate University. I'd survived eleven seasons in a profession where the average longevity for a player is six. I'd become the Seattle Seahawks' all-time leader in tackles and was second all-time on the team in interceptions. I'd been blessed with the respect of my peers, who voted me into the Pro Bowl twice.

When my eleventh season with the Seahawks ended, there was no question in my mind that God had brought me to Seattle and that he had blessed me tremendously while I was there. I was grateful for that, and if my pro football career had ended right then, I wouldn't have felt bitter or slighted, but grateful for what God had given me and grateful to the Seattle community and the Seahawks organization for a great ride.

I'm not going to tell you I wasn't concerned about my future following the 1995 season. I believe that we're supposed to concern ourselves with those things. I believe we're supposed to set goals and make plans, all the time realizing that it's God who guides our steps. I was ready and willing to go where he wanted me to go, even if that meant leaving football. I knew I could still play and contribute on a team—be it the Seahawks or somebody else.

As the summer of 1996 wore on, it looked more and more like I might be traded or cut. I still had a year left on my contract with the Seahawks, and I would have been free to sign with anybody after the 1996 season. But Coach Erickson had made it obvious to everyone that a change was going to be made when he signed Darryl Williams, a free agent from the Cincinnati Bengals who had played collegiately for him at the University of Miami, to a four-year contract. Somebody had to go, and it looked like it was going to be me.

The thought of leaving Seattle hurt, but at the same time I didn't take it personally. After eleven years in the league, I understood this was business and that the Seahawks were obligated first to do what was best for their organization. But I wanted the Seahawks to make their move soon so I could get on with my life.

After the Seahawks signed Darryl Williams, I told them, "Look, you're not going to hurt my feelings if you trade me. If I'm not your guy, just say so. If you don't want me to play for you, I'm not bitter. Go ahead and trade me."

At that point, they gave me some options, one of which was to stay in Seattle and take a pay cut. Another option was to cut me and let me try to sign with another team. The final option was to trade me.

I was told that the Seahawks would do what I wanted, but I knew they were going to do what was best for them. I knew that if it was best for them to simply cut me, that's what they'd do. It bothered me to be told it was up to me, but I kept it to myself. I wasn't going to appear angry or bitter.

Right around that time I got a call from Reggie White, who had become a friend of mine over the previous few years. He told me, "I'm praying for you, Eugene." I knew what Reggie meant: He was praying that the door would be opened for me to come to Green Bay and play for the Packers. After talking to Reggie, I told Gia, "I think God's going to move us to Green Bay."

Going to Green Bay sounded like a good option to me. It was a team that had a chance not just to go to the play-offs, but to contend for the Super Bowl. The Packers had gone to the National Football Conference Championship game the previous season, losing to the eventual Super Bowl champion Dallas Cowboys. The year before that, they'd lost to the Cowboys in an NFC divisional play-off game. It seemed like the Packers were going through a progression: first, they make the play-offs, next they lose in a divisional play-off game, then they make it to the conference championship. It seemed only logical that they were on their way to the Super Bowl.

Still, it seemed odd to me that Reggie would call me like that. What made him think the Packers were trying to trade for me? I went to the Seahawks and asked them about it.

"Is it true the Packers are interested in me?" I asked.

"No, we haven't talked to anybody."

I knew that couldn't be true. I knew that the Packers weren't allowed to contact me without the Seahawks' permission. I knew someone in Green Bay had been talking. Finally, I got the word from the Seahawks that they were entertaining a trade offer, but had no solid leads from the Packers—just some inquiries. It seemed that the Seahawks had found out that I had trade value, so they were trying to get something in return for me.

It's a strange feeling, knowing your team is trying to trade you. On one had, you realize that your team doesn't want you anymore. But on the other hand, someone does. On the whole, getting traded is far better than getting cut. It means that somebody wants you.

I wasn't worried about it. I knew that even if my career in the NFL was over, I could go on and do something else. Besides, I knew God was in control. I knew that he was going to take care of the situation and put me where he wanted me to be.

It turns out that the Packers did want me. Just weeks before training camp was to start, they sent Matt LaBounty, a veteran defensive end, to Seattle to get me. My time with the Seahawks was now over. My wife and kids and I would be moving to Green Bay, Wisconsin.

When I left the Seahawks I still had friends in Seattle—on the team, as well as others—who were angry that I had been traded. The way they saw it, it wasn't right, the way the Seahawks treated me. I didn't see it that way, though. To me, it would have been a slap in the face of my God if I had allowed myself to be bitter or angry about being traded. He'd blessed me with eleven great years in Seattle, but now it was time for me to move on to a new phase in my life. I left with no hard feelings.

## Leaving a Legacy in Seattle

When I think of the blessings I received while I was a member of the Seattle Seahawks, I can't help but praise God for using me in the lives of the men I knew when I was there and for using the men of God I met there in my life, too. It was through these people that God has built a legacy with the Seahawks, a legacy that will continue many, many years after I've been gone.

I enjoyed the fellowship of great brothers in Christ with the Seahawks—Dave Brown, Jeff Kemp, Steve Largent, John Kasay, and many others. God had used me to help change the lives of some of my teammates, and he had used some of my teammates—particularly Dave Brown—to change my life.

I believe God wants to use people who love him to build a legacy wherever they are planted. I believe that I am part of God's legacy in Seattle, a legacy that was passed through me by Dave Brown. Dave wasn't just one of the best football players I've ever played with, he's also a man of God who did more to shape my walk with Christ than anybody I've known since I came into the league.

It wasn't always easy to have him as my mentor—my discipler. It took endurance to get through some of the things he gently, firmly, and lovingly put me through. But the results are unmistakable. I have no idea how many people Dave and I influenced for Jesus Christ since I've known him. We planted seeds in men's hearts, led men in the Sinner's Prayer, and encouraged those who knew God but were struggling. And I continued those things after Dave Brown left Seattle to play for the Green Bay Packers.

I'll never forget how Dave Brown took me aside and told me that I would be next on the team to uphold the Word of God. Dave was an elder at

Antioch Bible Church in Kirkland, Washington, and he laid his hand on me, anointed me with oil, prayed for me, and told me what I would be doing with the team. Dave passed me the torch, and when I left the Seahawks, I passed it on to another player, Todd Peterson. I put my hand on Todd and said, "You're God's man. Uphold his Word on this team. Go do it!"

It's beautiful to me to see how God passes his legacy from one person to the next. And it was beautiful to me how he used a white man and a black man as spiritual leaders of the team. When I first came, we had Dave Brown and Steve Largent. When they left, there was me and Jeff Kemp, then John Kasay, then Todd Peterson. I believed then and I believe now that there was a purpose for that. It gave us a chance to love one another and be reconciled as brothers in the Lord—in front of the whole team. It gave us a chance to show the men on our team that differences in race meant nothing when compared with the bond that existed between us as men of God. We were living demonstrations of what Galatians 3:28 says: "There is neither Jew nor Greek, slave nor free, male nor female, for you are all one in Christ Jesus."

Our ministry went on regardless of the team's circumstances. We always had our team Bible studies, prayer meetings, and chapel services. Even in the midst of our 2–14 season, we continued to praise God and serve him, demonstrating to everybody on the team that God would be glorified, even in the midst of what other people considered failure.

God used me all eleven years I played for the Seattle Seahawks, but he never stopped teaching me and helping me to grow in my relationship with him and with others on the team. One of the most memorable lessons I learned was during my first four or five years with the team, when Jeff Kemp was with the team as a backup quarterback. I felt frustrated because I didn't think Chuck Knox appreciated my contribution to the team, that I wasn't performing well enough to satisfy him. One day, I was talking to Jeff and my wife about it—complaining is more like it—and he made a suggestion: "Eugene, why don't you pray for Chuck? When you feel angry at him, pray for him."

It wasn't easy. My flesh fought against that, but I still did it. When I had bad feelings for Chuck Knox or when I felt frustrated at him, I prayed for him. It worked, too. No, God didn't change Chuck Knox. That wasn't his objective anyway. He changed me. He got my eyes off me and on glorifying him. Soon, my attitude about Coach Knox changed. I grew to love the man. Where before I had feelings of resentment toward him, I now feel a sense of love for the man and gratitude toward him for helping give me the opportunity to do what I've done in the NFL.

That attitude was extended toward the Seahawks, too, even as I prepared to leave the team and move on to a new phase of my professional football career. I left without bitterness or anger, but with a feeling of gratitude for a great eleven years in a beautiful city and with some great men of God.

Now, it was time for me to help build a new legacy with the Green Bay Packers.

## The Start of Something Special

When you talk about legacies on professional football teams, you have to think of the Green Bay Packers. When I first joined the team, I was told that it would be in my best interests for me to know a little something about the history of the team that was based in what had affectionately come to be known as "Titletown."

There is a feeling of pride among Packer players, a feeling that they are stewards of a great football legacy left behind for them by players such as Bart Starr, Ray Nitschke, Paul Hornung, Willie Davis, Jim Taylor, Don Hutson, and Jerry Kramer, just to name a few.

The Packers have, to say the least, a prominent place in professional football history. When I first arrived in Green Bay, the Packers had won eleven world championships, including the first two Super Bowls—in 1966 and 1967, under legendary coach Vince Lombardi.

When I came to Green Bay, it looked like they were on their way to a return to the Super Bowl. I looked forward to being a part of something special.

I'm not sure what the Green Bay Packers expected of me when I arrived at training camp during the summer of 1996. My impression is that they thought they were getting an old guy—I was thirty-three at the time—who was at the end of his career and who was coming off an Achilles tendon injury. I'm sure they were thinking of me as old for a professional football player and as slightly damaged goods because of my injury. Still, I knew they expected me to come in and start and play maybe a year or two. I don't think they expected me to be all that effective—just serviceable.

I had to change my approach that season as I headed into training camp. I had to prove myself all over again. The Seahawks had been down for the last few years I was with them, so I knew none of the coaches at Green Bay had seen much of me. I wanted to go out those first few days of training camp and get something out of the way: I wanted to show them that this thirty-three-year-old veteran with the surgically repaired Achilles tendon could hit, run, and catch the football. I wanted to show them what I could do during my first few days of camp, then get down to the business of playing football.

*They think they're getting an old guy who's at the end of his career,* I thought. *They're going to be plenty surprised. I've got to show them what I can do. Let me hit somebody really hard and see what they think.*

I settled all that during the first day at training camp. I blasted one of their running backs, then later made an interception. I left no question in anybody's minds that I could still play. Within a short time, I had shown the coaches and players that I wasn't going to just be taking up space on the field with the defense; I was going to contribute—more than the Packers probably expected when they traded for me.

The Packers were a team full of great players—guys who could flat out get it done on the football field. Not only that, they were strong people and natural leaders. I soon fit right in, establishing myself as one of the leaders—spiritual and emotional—on the team. Guys like Reggie White, Brett Favre, LeRoy Butler, Wayne Simmons, Frank Winters, and Shawn Jones—all of them were men who could lead, whose confidence was contagious. They could all make big plays, spectacular plays. But they led in how they did it within the confines of the team game. They didn't need their egos massaged, and they weren't caught up in their own statistics. They were selfless football players.

And I jumped right in and established leadership of my own, leadership that complemented that of the men who had been there before me. It didn't take me long to see what was happening there in Green Bay.

This was going to be one special season!

## SERVING GOD WITH THE PACKERS

# PLAYING OUT THE FAITH ON THE FOOTBALL FIELD

was amazed when I first got to Green Bay at how many members of the Packers truly loved God and were committed to serving him. There was Reggie White, Don Beebe, Keith Jackson, Robert Brooks (I called him MOG, short for Man of God), Adam Timmerman, John Michels, Kenny Ruettgers...the list goes on.

That is what made my time with the Green Bay Packers so special. It was a time when I saw Christian brothers encourage one another and build up one another in the faith, when I saw nonbelievers receiving the Word of God from those of us who believed, and when I saw Christianity being played out week after week, month after month, within the setting of a professional football team.

To me, professional football, while it is ultimately just a game, is also a microcosm of the real world. It is a place where guys' problems are played out on the setting of a football field, a training room, and a locker room. Football players have the same kinds of problems as anybody else. They have family problems, marital problems, and, if you can believe this, money problems like everybody else.

Most of all, they need Jesus Christ like everybody else. It has been my privilege to be used of God to take my faith to the National Football League to share Jesus Christ with a group of men who are like the rest of the world: lost in their sin and on their way to an eternity apart from a living God who loves them more than they can imagine.

## Sharing the Faith—Openly

Talking about Jesus was commonplace with the Packers. It wasn't in whispered tones, either. It was out in the open for everybody to hear. Guys would talk about Jesus out loud and without hesitation. They'd talk about what God was doing in their lives, what they'd heard in church, or what they'd read in the Bible. All the believers on the team talked that way, and soon even those who hadn't put their trust in Christ talked openly about God.

It was an atmosphere where, largely because of Coach Mike Holmgren, we were able to openly express ourselves. As the team's head coach, Mike realized he couldn't speak as forcefully on the subject as we could. He knew he had to be careful how he used that position. But Mike is also a man who loves God, and he was sympathetic to the propagation of the gospel in our locker room. I'll say it now, God used Mike Holmgren with the Packers. Maybe Mike couldn't stand up in the locker room like I could or Reggie White could, but he knew there were ringleaders on the team, strong men of God who could do the work that God had called us to do.

And that work started where I believe any good works for God should start: with prayer and reading and study of the Word.

## Seeking God in a Team Setting

Reggie White was one of the ringleaders on the Packers when it came to prayer and Bible study. And because of the tremendous respect guys have for Reggie, when he called a prayer meeting or Bible study, guys were there— even the nonbelievers. It was not uncommon when Reggie called a prayer meeting to have thirty people show up, whether it was held in the weight room or the shower. "Team prayer! We're going to go have team prayer!" Reggie would call out in his deep, gravely voice, then we'd all get together, join hands, and pray.

We'd pray before games, after games, after practice. We'd pray for guys' individual needs. We'd pray for the health and safety of our teammates and opponents and we'd pray that God would be glorified in everything we did on and off the field. Sometimes we'd pray for one another's injuries. I was once the beneficiary of that kind of prayer.

During my first season in Green Bay, I had injured my ankle during our 28–18 win over Detroit at Lambeau Field. I played hurt in our next game at Kansas City. We had a key game coming up the following week against the Dallas Cowboys at Texas Stadium, and I didn't want to miss it. Sean Jones, our starting defensive end, was hurt and Robert Brooks was out for the season with a knee injury. I didn't want to add to the team's injury problems.

One day I was sitting in the training room getting my ankle worked on, and Reggie White looked at me and said, "Look here, Gene, come on in the next room when you're done here, and we're going to have some prayer time."

"Okay, Reg," I said. "I'll be right over."

I hobbled out of the training room to where Reggie and some of the other believers on the team were waiting for me. Reggie anointed my foot with oil, and the guys laid hands on me and started praying that my ankle would be healed. Right there in the Packers' training facility—in the middle of all the modern, conventional medicine available to a player—I sat as a group of men laid their hands on me and asked God to heal me.

To me, this was Christianity in action. This was real life. This was people meeting the needs of their brothers who were going through life's trials by taking them to the Lord in prayer. It was guys applying their faith to our current situation.

We prayed a lot for guys who were injured, and that made a big impression, especially on guys who weren't believers. When we prayed, guys would push in to get prayed for, saying, "Let me get in there, man! Pray for me too! Pray for my shoulder, man. Pray that God will heal my knee!" They wanted us, the men of God on the Packers, to be advocates for them, to be mediators.

When guys were faced with problems—injuries, personal problems, financial difficulties…you name it—it was only a matter of time before they came to Reggie White, Don Beebe, Keith Jackson, Robert Brooks, or me for prayer and counsel. Why? It wasn't because we were perfect and had our lives perfectly together. It wasn't because any of us, outside of Christ, were anything special. It was because they could see in our lives that what we had was real, that we had the answers to life's problems, that we had a connection with the living God. They knew we had Jesus Christ.

## Time in the Word

The study of God's Word was important to us. We talked to one another about the Word constantly, and we had regular Bible studies, many of which were led by Reggie White. Reggie knew the Word of God, and he loved talking about it. He came to me often to use me as a sounding board for a Bible study he was preparing.

"Gene, I was getting ready for Bible study and I was going over the relationship of the Shepherd to the sheep," he'd say. "God has been teaching me some awesome things about that. What do you think?"

"I think that would be good, Reg," I'd tell him. "You could do that, but you also might want to take this perspective as well..."

It was incredible to see the kind of camaraderie and fellowship this group of believers on the Green Bay Packers had with one another. It was a situation where we were real with one another, where we looked to one another for prayer and support. And it was a situation where the Word of God was being presented to those around us, starting with our teammates.

## Taking Him to Our Teammates

One of the most important things I've learned about presenting the Word of God to people is that my responsibility ends there. God has commanded all of us to preach the gospel through our words and our deeds. After that, it's his responsibility to work in people's hearts.

I struggled with that early in my career in the National Football League. I can remember well feeling the frustration of seeing my teammates in Seattle living what I considered a "pseudo-Christianity." I used to get angry to the point of tears when I saw those who professed faith in Christ but whose lives didn't measure up to what I thought they should. I can remember one time asking my teammates in the locker room, "Doesn't anybody here fear God? Where is God on this team?" Guys looked at me like I was crazy.

What bothered me most was what I considered guys' wrong motivations for praying or hearing the Word of God. I felt like some of them wanted to pray and hear God's Word so that he would bless them and make them successful on the football field. Other than that, it didn't seem to me that they wanted much to do with God.

Since that time, I've learned something important about other men's motivations for praying and hearing the Word: It's none of my business! Now, I don't really care what their motivation is, only that guys have an opportunity to have God speak to their hearts when they hear the Word. I've learned that I don't have to worry about whether the Word is taking root in a man's heart. That's God's responsibility. My job is to proclaim the Word of God, pray, and let God be God—let him worry about the results.

Once I grasped that concept, my ministry with my teammates blossomed, and I grew spiritually and became more effective in proclaiming the Word. I became more tolerant of people because I remembered that prior to 1984, when God arrested my way of thinking and living, I didn't approach God with the right motives, either. Realizing that allowed me to become more tolerant of people and able to give them more latitude and forgiveness.

Now, I don't care why people ask me to pray for them. I don't care if they are asking for prayer because they want to win a football game, because they're negotiating a new contract, or if they're trying to work out a problem with their wives.

I don't care why guys go to chapel or mass before the game, either. One day, about four hours before a road game, I counted twenty-five or so people at chapel, then another thirty or so at mass. That's more than fifty-five guys hearing the Word of God before the game. That's out of about eighty-five who travel with the team—including players, coaches, and training staff. Why do these guys all go to a service? Some go because they truly love God, others because they want a good-luck charm for the game or because it's just tradition to go to chapel.

I'm not the Holy Spirit, and it's not my job to search their hearts. All I know is that the Word of God doesn't return void.

I still smile—even laugh a little—when I think of a great example of this that I saw in Green Bay.

## You're Brangin' It!

We had a little saying with the Packers we'd use when someone did something really well. When someone made a great play, we'd say, "Baby, you're brangin' it!" In other words, "You're bringin' it!" or, "Well done!"

I heard this several times from a group of guys who were some of the meanest, hardest-hitting players on the team: the linebackers—Wayne Simmons, Brian Williams, George Koonce, Lamont Hollinquest, Bernardo Harris, and the rest of them. They wouldn't go on the field for a game unless Keith Jackson, our starting tight end, prayed for them.

We'd be ready to head out to the field after our team prayer when the linebackers would call out, "Hey, Keith! Get over here and pray for us!" Keith would always walk over to the linebackers, then say, "I need someone to come here and in the name of the Lord agree with me and my brothers." That meant it was time for me and Reggie White to come over and lay hands on them while Keith prayed. Then Keith Jackson would start praying a beautiful, psalmlike, Martin Luther King-type prayer:

"Lord, we know you can do all things. We know that everything belongs in your hands. There's nothing out of your control. Father, you created the heavens and the earth. Everything we see and everything we don't see…"

As Keith is praying, Reggie and I are agreeing with him: "Yes, Lord! Amen! In Jesus' name…" Meanwhile, the linebackers, in their own way, are also agreeing: "Yeah! That's right! That's you God!"

"…Father, in the name of the Lord Jesus Christ, we ask you to go with these brothers today, that you lay your hand of protection on them, that you glorify yourself in all that they do and say today. In Jesus' name! In Jesus' name! In Jesus' name! And everybody who agrees says…"

"AMEN!"

It was a beautiful prayer, and every time it drew to an end, one of the linebackers, the same one every time, would swear, look up at Keith and say, "You are brangin' it!" which in his own words meant, "Thank you for that beautiful prayer!"

I don't condone cursing or taking the Lord's name in vain, but I smiled every time we finished that prayer. There was something slightly humorous about this linebacker cursing to let us know how much he appreciated us praying for him and his buddies. I realized that he wasn't trying to be blasphemous or sacrilegious. He was expressing his appreciation in a way that was familiar to him. It didn't greatly offend me to hear this man use those words. The way I saw it, he wasn't living right anyway. To me, there was a certain amount of innocence in that.

More than that, though, I realized that God was there, in the presence of this swearing, simply because Keith Jackson, Reggie White, and myself were there agreeing in Jesus' name. I remember thinking to myself, *Lord, I don't know what you're doing in my man's heart. All I know is that dude's hearing the Word of God, and you said your Word would not return to you void. I'm not even concerned about his response. All I know is that if you get hold of that man, then you'll take all the cursing and blaspheming and taking the Lord's name in vain and you'll change him and make him new, because that's what you promised to do. Old things will be passed away, all things will become new. I don't care what his response is. I'm just glad he's there hearing that prayer.*

God never appointed me to be a moral policeman or to keep track of how other people talk. He just told me to proclaim the Word of God wherever I am and whatever I'm doing. When I come in contact with guys who don't know God, I don't try to tell them to change the way they talk or the way they act. I've had guys say to me, "I really need to quit cursing so much," or "I need to change the way I'm living." I always tell them, "You just need Jesus Christ." I tell them that because I know that the first thing God does in someone's life is renew them spiritually. Then he starts changing the way they live.

I love allowing people to hear the Word of God when they ask me to pray for them. To me, that's their first step toward the kingdom of God. God will take care of all the junk in their lives in his time. I'm just glad that there are guys willing to listen to the Word when they ask me to pray for them. To me, getting guys to hear the Word is a lot like getting your dog to play checkers. You wouldn't get mad when the dog didn't make the right move; you'd be happy because he's playing checkers at all. You can teach him the right moves later.

## A Unique Position

I believe that anybody who is willing can be used of God in his own unique situation. In my case—and in the case of guys like Don Beebe, Reggie White, Keith Jackson, and the rest—God has put me in a position where I can influence men in the National Football League.

There are guys in the NFL who, if they are going to hear the Word of God, will need to hear it from someone like myself or Reggie White or Robert Brooks—their peers in the league. That is a platform that is given to very few men. It's a platform that allows them to reach some hard, tough men—men who won't listen to anybody else.

That is the kind of influence God has given me. Playing in the NFL has allowed me to minister to more players than I can count, but it also gives me many opportunities to reach out to those who are outside my professional world.

## To the Outer Reaches

It has always amazed me how many people will listen to me just because I play pro football. People who wouldn't otherwise give me the time of day want to hear what I have to say just because I get paid to play a kids' game. It was like that to the extreme when I played for the Packers. The people in that city love each and every member of the Packers and listen to anything a member of the team has to say. That was amazing to me, but what is even more amazing is the number of people God brings into my life so that he can use me to minister to them.

One of my most memorable examples of this involved a young man I can't wait to see when I get to heaven. His name was Jedidiah, and he had terminal cancer. Jedidiah called the Packers' public relations office just before Super Bowl XXXI wanting to talk to one of the players. One of the women in that office contacted me and said, "I was looking for Reggie White to take this call, but I can't find him. Would you talk to this guy? He loves the Packers. Maybe you could cheer him up a little bit." I said, "Okay. I'll talk to the guy."

I went to the Packers' ticket office and called him. Immediately, I could hear in his voice just how sick he was. I could hear over the phone that it was a major effort just to talk. He was no older than eighteen, but his body had been so ravaged by the cancer that he was left without strength to do even the most basic things.

"Hey Jedidiah, how ya doin'?" I said. "This is Eugene Robinson with the Packers."

"The Packers! Man, I love the Packers!" he said, his voice rising in enthusiasm despite his sickness. "The Packers are my favorite team!"

"We're getting ready to go down to the Super Bowl and do our thing."

"Man that's great! How's Brett? How about Reggie? You guys'll win for sure."

We talked about football for a while, then I felt that prompting in my heart: I needed to talk to this young man about Jesus Christ.

I said, "Hey Jedidiah, do you know Jesus?"

"No! What about him?"

"Listen Jedidiah, I want to share something with you. We've been talking about superficial stuff. Obviously I've been given your name for a reason. Let me tell you about Jesus Christ."

I told Jedidiah that God wanted to have peace with him, but that there was a problem called sin. I told him the remedy for that problem is Jesus Christ, but that it's not enough to know that—he needed to respond to Jesus Christ and have a personal relationship with him.

Finally, I said, "Jedidiah, would you like to know Jesus as your personal Lord and Savior?"

I'll never forget the fervor, the passion in his voice when he answered me. I still get emotional when I think of that conversation. Jedidiah was quiet for a moment, then said, "Yeah! YEAH! That's what I want! That's exactly what I want. I want Jesus!"

The impact of the Word of God had rushed Jedidiah. The Holy Spirit of God was working in this young man's heart, convicting him of his need for the Savior.

"You've already settled in your heart what you want to do," I said. "Let me lead you in a prayer. It's called the Sinner's Prayer. Why don't you repeat after me: 'God, I'm a sinner. I thank you for sending Jesus Christ to die for my sins. Thank you for sending him to die for the forgiveness of my sins. I want to follow him and make him the Lord of my life. God, I accept him into my heart right now. I choose to invite him into my life right now. And I pray that you'll make me the person you intended me to be. Thank you for coming into my life. Amen.'"

I talked to Jedidiah for a while longer, then told him I'd call him again after I got back from the Super Bowl. When I called Jedidiah's home a few weeks later, his sister answered the phone.

"This is Eugene Robinson. I'm calling for Jedidiah."

"I want to thank you for talking to my brother," she said, as her voice started to tremble. Then she told me the bittersweet news: Jedidiah had passed away. I felt heartbroken that I wouldn't get a chance to talk to him, but at the same time I rejoiced because I knew where he was and that I would see him again.

"My family wants to thank you for what you shared with Jedidiah," she said. "It meant a lot to him." About a week later, I received a letter from his family talking about Jedidiah and his battle with cancer. They told me how much they appreciated my calling him.

The Bible tells us that God will reward each of us who are faithful in serving him while we're here on earth. I rejoice in that, but I also realize that one of the best rewards for me when I get there will be to see Jedidiah—the new Jedidiah, complete with a new body that will never age or be subject to the ravages of cancer or any other disease.

## Why Me?

I've wondered sometimes why God uses me, why he would take my position as a football player and use it to bring people to himself. The answer that comes back is a simple one: because I am available.

It's impossible for me to know why God elevated me in the eyes of men as a member of a Super Bowl championship team. Why he didn't elevate someone else is a mystery I probably won't understand until I'm in heaven. All I know is that he has a purpose for my life, both on and off the field.

God *did* elevate me. He *did* allow me to play well over a decade in the NFL, to be named to two Pro Bowls, and to play for a Super Bowl champion-ship team. I know God won't put other people in the position he put me in. I know there are thousands of young men out there who have dreams of doing what I've done, but who will never receive the opportunity. When I think about the blessings I've received from God in my career, I can't help but feel a wave of gratitude.

I've had a great time playing in the National Football League, but it's a lot more to me than just a job I enjoy. To me, the best part of my being blessed with a career in the NFL is that I get to use my position to further the gospel of Jesus Christ. I can use the fact that people want to hear what I have to say simply because I play football to tell them that God loves them, that he has made a way for them to have eternal fellowship with him.

When someone hears what I have to say and downplays it by referring to me as "deeply religious," I tell them, "No, I'm not religious. I'm a Christian. I have a relationship with God through his Son, Jesus Christ, and he gives me the strength to do the things I've done. Apart from him I can do nothing."

That's the message people need to hear. My teammates need to hear it. The people who approach me for an autograph or just to say hello need to hear it. The reporters I talk to need to hear it. The people who watch me on TV need to hear it.

It's a message we all need to hear. And it's a message I love to speak.

I thank God for allowing me to speak that message while playing with a great football team.

That made enduring everything I have to get where I am worth it!

## CHAPTER ELEVEN

**INSIDE THE HYPE**

# ENJOYING A SUPER BOWL SEASON

The 1996 Green Bay Packers were a team that will someday be well represented in the kingdom of God. We had a team full of guys who loved God and who served him in everything they did.

But there was something else about the Packers, something that the whole world of football already knows: We could play the game of football!

When I look back at that team, I see a group of guys who could play the game. On offense, we had the best quarterback in the National Football League, Brett Favre. We had Dorsey Levens and Edgar Bennett at running back and William Henderson at fullback. We had Antonio Freeman and, later (after Robert Brooks was injured), Andre Rison as wide receivers. Our offensive linemen could all play. On defense, we had one of the best front fours in the game, with Reggie White and Sean Jones at the ends and Gabe Wilkins and Santana Dotson at the tackles. Our linebackers—George Koonce (before he was injured), Brian Williams, Wayne Simmons, and Ron Cox could play. Defensive backs LeRoy Butler, Doug Evans, and Craig Newsome could flat out play the game.

It was a great team I joined that season, solid at every position. It was also a team that had the attitude that we were going to win. That attitude started with guys like Brett Favre and Reggie White, and it was contagious. It was an attitude that when our offense got in the red zone, we were going to score 7 and not settle for a field goal. It was an attitude that our defense was going to stop people.

Were we cocky or arrogant? I don't think so. I believe we just had confidence in ourselves and in one another that we were going to succeed. It was a fun team to play for, but it was also a serious team. We joked around in the locker room and had fun with one another, but when it was time to play we got after it.

## A Great Season

The Green Bay Packers weren't overwhelming favorites to win the Super Bowl heading into the 1996 season. We, along with Dallas and San Francisco, were considered the class of the National Football Conference.

Everybody knew we'd be good, probably a Super Bowl contender, but I don't think a lot of people realized just how good we were going to be. Nobody had any idea that we would have by far the best defense in the league *and* the top-scoring offense. That's right, we led the league in scoring defense *and* scoring offense.

During the first three weeks of the 1996 season, the Packers looked untouchable. We won all three of our games by a combined score of 115–26. After a 30–21 loss to the Minnesota Vikings at the Metrodome, we continued on our rampage, beating Seattle 31–10 and Chicago 37–6 in a pair of road games.

Through nine games, we were 8–1, but we went into what some people might call a minislump after that, losing at Kansas City and Dallas on a *Monday Night Football* game for our only back-to-back losses of the season. The loss to Dallas was especially hard for us to take, because the Cowboys had dropped the Packers out of the play-offs the previous two seasons and had beaten Green Bay seven straight times. We knew we would probably have to beat the Cowboys to get to the Super Bowl, and our 21–6 loss that night made us realize that we still had work to do.

After our loss to the Cowboys, we blew through our final five games to finish 13–3, setting a team record for most wins in a season. It was a great season for the Packers, and a great one for me personally. I finished the season with a team-high 6 interceptions while finishing fourth on the club in tackles. And when the regular season was over, it was time for me to take part in something I hadn't been a part of since the 1988 season: the NFL play-offs.

## It Can't Be This Easy

When the 1996 play-offs started, there was no question who was the favorite to represent the NFC in the Super Bowl (and, by the way, blow out the American Football Conference representative). The Packers had just finished a brilliant season, a season in which they again caught the attention of the American public.

We didn't mind being looked at as the team to beat, but we knew we needed to be ready for what would be coming the next few weeks. The NFL play-offs are a one-shot deal. You lose once and you're out. In all the other major professional sports leagues, you can have one bad game and still advance to the next round because the play-offs are all in series. In football, though, it's one loss and you're headed home.

We knew that we had to come out with our best every game if we wanted to win the Super Bowl. That's exactly what we did, too. Even though there was so much more at stake in each game, we came out in the play-offs with the same kind of confidence we had during the regular season.

We were dominating in the play-offs—first in a 35–14 blowout of the San Francisco 49ers in a divisional play-off game, then in a 30–13 win over the upstart Carolina Panthers in the NFC championship game.

We got off to a quick start against the 49ers, as Desmond Howard returned 49er punter Tommy Thompson's first kick 71 yards for a touchdown, then returned the second San Francisco punt 46 yards to the 49ers 7-yard line to set up a touchdown pass from Brett Favre to Andre Rison. That made it 14–0, and we went up 21–0 in the second quarter when Edgar Bennett ran 2 yards up the middle for our third touchdown.

The 49ers rallied to make it 21–14 on two quick touchdowns following turnovers, but our offense responded with a methodical 72-yard drive for a touchdown. (Antonio Freeman recovered Edgar Bennett's fumble in the end zone for the score.) Edgar scored again on an 11-yard run with just over five minutes left in the game to seal it for us.

I had not one, but two punctuation marks at the end of the game in the form of a pair of interceptions from 49er quarterback Elvis Grbac. (I would have had a third pick that game, but a penalty on the 49er offense negated an interception.)

We didn't get off to a great start against the Panthers, who had come out of nowhere as a second-year franchise to first make the play-offs, then advance to the NFC championship game with their stunning 26–17 win over the Dallas Cowboys in the divisional play-off game at Texas Stadium. We fell behind 7–0, then 10–7 after two early turnovers.

After getting the mistakes out of our systems, we went on to blow out the Panthers, taking a 27–13 lead late in the third quarter and putting the game pretty much out of reach. Dorsey Levens and Brett Favre had great days, and our defense shut down Carolina, holding the Panthers to 45 yards rushing for the game.

The Green Bay Packers had taken that next step toward supremacy in the National Football League. We went from also-rans in the Super Bowl derby to earning a place in the Big Game. We had accomplished one of our biggest goals of the season with our win over Carolina. But we weren't finished yet. We had one more hill to climb before we could call it a season.

We were looking to beat the AFC champion New England Patriots in Super Bowl XXXI.

But first, we were going to have to endure that two weeks of hype leading up to that annual event known as Super Bowl Sunday.

## A Crazy Week

The week of the Super Bowl is like no week I've ever known. It's a week of incredible hype and media attention. The hype is so intense that it's easy for players to forget for a moment why they're there: to play for the world championship of professional football.

It's a week where the newspapers, magazines, and radio and television networks cover the upcoming game from every conceivable angle. There is a special day that has come to be known as Media Day where all the reporters and writers converged on New Orleans to meet with the players at the stadium to get their scoops. On that day, there were, I would guess, upwards of

INSIDE THE HYPE

two thousand people, talking to players and getting every perspective on the game. During that time, players and coaches talk to reporters from every state of the union as well as many other countries.

It's tough to practice much the week before the Super Bowl, but that's not all bad. By the time you get to that point, you're honing the things you've done all year. You've already seen countless hours of film of your opponent, and you know what you're going to do come game time. If you aren't to that point, you're in trouble because there are just too many distractions. Between media days, meetings, and the long list of Super Bowl events, you just don't have the luxury of extra time to practice.

We arrived in New Orleans the Sunday before the game, leaving behind our wives and kids, who joined us later that week. Those first four or five days were a time when we dealt with the media, held team meetings, and spent some free time in the city.

## Kickin' It in the Big Easy

Mike Holmgren had a curfew for us, and it was a good thing. In a big city like New Orleans, guys will stay out all night long if you let them. That could have been an added distraction, especially in a place like New Orleans, which is well known for its night life.

I didn't stay out too late that week, but I had a chance to visit a jazz club in New Orleans, and it turned out to be one of the most memorable moments of that week. I was with Keith Jackson at the club, and we were enjoying a good meal and some live jazz.

When it comes to music, give me jazz. I have a good collection of jazz CDs at home, and I started playing the saxophone in 1986. I knew when we went to New Orleans for the Super Bowl that I was going to a jazz club some-time that week. Now, here we were, having a great time, when one of the musicians started walking around the place playing his soprano saxophone. It was really melodic and smooth, almost like a slow ballad. I started talking with the guy when he got close to our table.

"Man, what key are you playing in?" I asked him.

**123**

"I'm playing in the key of A," he said. "Do you play the saxophone?"

"Yeah I do. Do you mind if I grab your horn?"

He handed me the sax, and I started to play. Nobody in the band knew it was me playing. I was just improvising, trying to keep up with the band, when several of my teammates who had come to the same club realized it was me playing.

"Go Gene-O! Go Gene-O! That's my boy! Turn it out, Gene-O!" they called out. They were dancing and giving each other high fives.

It was a great break for me and Keith. For one night, we weren't football players, just a couple of guys who liked good music. We'd been getting inundated with football all that morning and afternoon, and it was good to get out for a night, away from the media frenzy and away from living, eating, and breathing football.

It was a great night for us, but when it was over it was back to football.

## Final Preparations

By the time Thursday rolls around, you've done and said just about everything you can to be ready for the Super Bowl. At that point, the hay's in the barn. There is literally nothing more that can be done to get yourself ready—at least from the football standpoint.

I spent Saturday with my wife and kids. That evening we went back to the hotel, and I spent some time in some final team meetings where we talked—not so much about strategy or what we were going to do, but about our motivation for playing. It couldn't have come at a better time.

That night, Mike Holmgren got up at our meeting and talked to us about motivation. Mike is a solid man, a Christian man who understands proper motivation. That night, for the first time I can remember, Mike wore his Super Bowl XXIV championship ring, which he earned as the offensive coordinator of the San Francisco 49ers. Mike made sure we could see it as it flashed and shined in the overhead lights.

"Some of you guys will be motivated to play for a Super Bowl ring," he said, then turned and lifted a blanket off a table in the room, revealing

$100,000 in cash. "Some of you guys might be playing for $100,000."

You could hear guys talking among themselves about the rings and the money. "Some of you guys might be playing for the Lombardi Trophy," Mike continued, as the room went dead silent. "Whatever you're playing for, we have an opportunity that most people will never have—to play in a Super Bowl. We have to seize the moment."

I thought about what Mike said as the meeting drew to a close. I thought about my motivation for playing. I thought about how I wanted to win the game, how I wanted to be a member of the best team in football. I thought about seizing this moment, a moment I may never see again. And I thought about glorifying God.

Later that night, a bunch of the players held a meeting we'd come to call Saturday Night Live. It's a time of prayer, talking about the Lord and his Word, and just talking about things. I was sitting there in that meeting with my teammates, and it hit me like a ton of bricks. I had to tell my teammates what was on my heart at that moment.

"You know what Coach said earlier about motivation?" I said. "Here's what God laid on my heart: We're not playing for a Super Bowl ring." I went on to tell them what Madeline Mims, who won a gold medal in the 1968 Summer Olympics in the 800, told me. "As she presented her gold medal to the Lord, she said, 'Lord, look what I've done. It's a gold medal for you, Lord.' The reply back from heaven was, 'Oh, gold…that's something we walk on up here.'

"And we're not playing for the $100,000. That's nice, and you can take care of your families with that, but we're not playing for that. Believe it or not, we're not playing for the Lombardi Trophy and all the prestige that it's going to get us.

"We're playing for a platform that we will have to share Jesus Christ with the world because we won a stupid football game. Everybody likes a winner. And because you won a game, somebody's going to throw a microphone in your face and say, 'How'd you do it? What did you guys do? What's going on?' They'll never see our Bible studies or the times when we pray together or when we talk about Jesus Christ with one another.

"We need to tell them that we're successful because we try to glorify God in all that we do. We're literally playing for the opportunity to share the gospel with a dying world because we won a football game. That's why we're playing this game."

I told my teammates that God can use us to glorify himself, and that he could use the New England Patriots. But whether we won or lost (to tell you the truth, I had an incredible confidence—almost a feeling of assurance—that we were going to win), God was going to be glorified. I told them that they needed to be ready to tell the reporters what motivated them. I told them not to be afraid to talk about what was on their hearts.

We prayed that night. We prayed that God would be glorified in what was about to happen, that his name would be lifted up by both teams. We prayed that people would be drawn to Jesus Christ because of what they saw in us on the football field and what they heard from us after the game.

That night—the night before the biggest football game of my life—I slept like a baby. I didn't sleep well the night before the NFC championship game or our first play-off game, but when the Super Bowl came around, I was so relaxed and ready to play that I slept like I didn't have a care in the world.

## Game Day

I woke up on January 26, 1997, as relaxed and confident in what was about to happen as I had been all that week. I was looking forward to what was going to transpire that day. As strange as it may sound, I just wasn't overwhelmed by what was going on.

I got up, got dressed, and went to the team breakfast, which was mandatory, even for guys who don't eat. Coach Holmgren wanted to get the day with the team started right, and he insisted that all of us be at breakfast, even if we just had a cup of coffee. He wanted everybody to start the day together. After some morning team meetings, we headed out to the Superdome about three hours before game time. Some of the guys got there earlier, but not me. I got there at the latest time I could. (I'd have arrived right at game time if I could have gotten away with it.)

I also don't dress early for games, and I don't follow any pattern when I dress. A lot of guys have their own rituals, where they do everything the same way and at the same time each game. Not me, not even for the Super Bowl. It takes me about ten minutes to get dressed, and I wait until about ten minutes before it's time for the team to go out on the field before I get dressed. Before that, I find a quiet place to listen to some music and work a crossword puzzle.

When I first started playing, I would go out on the field early to warm up, then come back in the locker room for the team prayer and last-minute instructions. Now, I wait until the last minute. I tell my teammates, "You all let me know when it's time to go out and warm up, okay." To me, dressing too early sets you up for a game of hurry up and wait.

When we went out on the field to warm up, the Superdome was already filled close to capacity. People want to get there early and soak in every moment of the Super Bowl hype. We warmed up, then went back inside and waited those last few minutes before the player introductions and the national anthem. Matt Millen, who played in a couple of Super Bowls for the Raiders before moving on to work as an analyst with one of the major television networks, had warned me before the game that there would be some dead time between the singing of the national anthem and player introductions and when we actually got down to the game. He told me to plan on relaxing for fifteen to twenty minutes between the ceremonies and the actual kickoff. It was great advice.

Luther Vandross, one of my favorite singers, came out and sang the national anthem that day in New Orleans. I love good singing, and Luther can bring it! When he finished, I was ready. I started to feel the butterflies in my stomach. It was a feeling of nervousness that I've grown to actually love. It's the feeling that tells me I'm mentally ready to play the game.

With all the hype, all the meetings, all the questions, and all the planning behind us, it was time to go. It was time to play the game. We went out that day, and we glorified our God in what we were doing.

And, by the way, we also won Super Bowl XXXI.

◄ **DEFENDING THE CROWN** ►

# TRYING TO REPEAT

**W**inning a Super Bowl isn't easy. It takes countless hours of hard work (before and during the season), supreme effort in every game, and a ton of endurance. As hard as it is to win a Super Bowl, it's even tougher to repeat. Every team looks forward to playing the champions, hoping for the chance to pull the upset. And make no mistake about it, any team on any given Sunday can knock off any other team.

We came into the 1997 preseason wearing the label of "favorite." The way we played the previous season gave every indication that we weren't a one-season wonder, that we were going to continue to be contenders. We returned from our Super Bowl championship season almost intact (one key loss was Super Bowl most valuable player Desmond Howard), and just about everybody was ready to fit us with a new set of rings before the season started.

We came into the season confident in our ability to repeat, but we knew the rest of the NFL wasn't about to roll over and let us walk to a second straight championship. We were going to have to earn it.

## A Slow Start

The Packers' 1997 preseason went pretty much the way the end of the regular season had in 1996: we were dominant. We finished the preseason with a 5–0 record, and it looked like we were ready to pick up where we had left off the previous January.

That didn't happen, though. We struggled to win our first regular season game—a 38–24 win over the Chicago Bears in a *Monday Night Football* game at Lambeau Field. The Bears actually outgained us that game and trailed by only a touchdown (18–11) at the half. I have to give them credit; they played tough all game long.

To make matters worse for us, we lost cornerback Craig Newsome for the season to a knee injury. Craig went down early in the game trying to cover Bears wide receiver Ricky Proehl. I felt terrible when I saw Craig go down. He was one of the hardest workers on the team, and, I believe, a future Pro Bowl player. He also wanted as badly as any of us to defend our Super Bowl championship. Now, instead of helping us achieve our goal of repeating this year, he would be facing a long period of rehabilitation, something no player looks forward to.

The injury to a key player notwithstanding, there was a lot of talk going around at that point in the season of us being the first team in NFL history to go 19–0 and the first to go undefeated since the 1972 Miami Dolphins, who went 17–0 on their way to a 14–7 win over the Washington Redskins in Super Bowl VII. LeRoy Butler talked openly about going 19–0, and that talk made the newspapers.

Realistically, I thought that someone along the way would rise up and knock us off. I knew that the Detroit Lions, who we were scheduled to play our fifth game of the season at the Silverdome, had a shot at beating us.

We didn't have to wait long to receive our first loss, however, as the Philadelphia Eagles beat us 10–9 at Veterans Stadium to drop us to 1–1. Our offense was out of sync all day long, and the Eagles played well defensively, keeping us from scoring a touchdown despite a 380–258 advantage in total yards. Suddenly, all that talk about going 19–0 was just an embarrassing memory.

The Packers continued to struggle, winning close games over the Dolphins and the Minnesota Vikings at Lambeau Field the next two weeks. The Vikings scared the daylights out of all of us after falling behind 31–7 at halftime. Minnesota pulled to within 31–22 on short touchdown passes from Brad Johnson to Cris Carter and Jake Reed. Minnesota had a chance to go ahead late in the game, but Johnson threw 3 straight incomplete passes after the Vikings had driven to our 46-yard line. That was a disturbing game. We were sloppy on defense. We should have won that game going away, but instead we barely held on.

All of the sudden, we were no longer the talk of the NFC Central Division. That honor was going to the Tampa Bay Buccaneers, who were 4–0. That with us heading into the game I was most concerned about when the season started.

## A Humbling in Detroit

Heading into our game with the Detroit Lions at the Pontiac Silverdome, the whole Green Bay Packers defense knew what the rest of the NFL was well aware of: to beat the Lions, you had to contain Barry Sanders.

I'll say it now, Barry Sanders is the best running back in the history of football. Jim Brown, O. J. Simpson, and Walter Payton were great, but Barry is at yet a higher level. Give me any superlative in the English language, and I'll use it to describe Barry Sanders.

Barry Sanders is strong, fast, quick, and has incredible vision. He accelerates through the hole so quickly that you can't get a hand on him, and if you do, he's strong enough to break tackles. I'm a good tackler, but Barry Sanders has made me look stupid. My son always points that out to me, too. He loves Barry Sanders. He always says, "Dad, you can't tackle Sanders." That may be true, but neither can anybody else.

Barry's a guy you hope you tackle. Many an NFL defensive player has a story about how Barry Sanders made them look like a Pop Warner player. I've got several, some of them when I was playing with Seattle and some with Green Bay. The most memorable came while I was with the Packers, in our fifth game of the 1997 season.

It was on a play where I was sure I would finally get a good shot at him. He had nowhere to go. There was a defender on his right side and on his left, and he was running through a little seam between the guys. He was headed upfield full speed, and I was closing in, ready to get a hit on him. *Finally*, I thought, *I've got him. I'm going to put a hit on Barry Sanders!*

I didn't think he could see me coming. We were headed at each other full speed, and I was ready for the collision. I got within a yard of him and prepared for the impact, when Barry made a cut…BACKWARDS! He was running full speed upfield, and he hit the brakes, stopped, and backed up one step, leaving me lunging at air. Barry headed back upfield, and he would have scored had LeRoy Butler not been backing me up. After pushing Barry out of bounds, LeRoy ran up to me, laughing. "Wait till you see this on the film, Gene!" he said. I couldn't wait.…

Barry Sanders had a huge game that day with 139 yards (actually, he had a lot of huge games that season, as he finished with 2,053 yards), and the Lions just plain whipped us 26–15. They played the game they had to in order to win.

We fell to a disappointing 3–2 on the season. What was worse was that Tampa Bay won that week to go 5–0 and take a two-game lead in the NFC Central. We were in a position of having to catch up. That with the Buccaneers heading north to meet us at Lambeau Field.

At last, The Battle of the Bays would mean something in the NFC Central standings.

## A Showdown at Lambeau

I don't know if anyone would have predicted that Tampa Bay would play the Packers in a game of such importance in the NFC Central Division standings. But I will tell you what I know: those guys are no joke! For years, the Tampa Bay Buccaneers were consistently one of the NFL's worst teams. But that changed when Coach Tony Dungy arrived prior to the 1996 season, giving the team new energy, new purpose.

The Buccaneers had ridden the running of rookie halfback Warrick Dunn and fullback Mike Alstott, the passing of Trent Dilfer, and a defense that featured players like Warren Sapp, Brad Culpepper, and Hardy Nickerson to their 5–0 start. They played hard and they played well.

We didn't have a great offensive game against the Buccaneers, but we had enough big plays, particularly in the second quarter, to pull out a 21–16 win.

Brett Favre threw two touchdown passes to Antonio Freeman in the second quarter and Gabe Wilkins made one of the biggest plays in the NFL that season when he picked off a Trent Dilfer pass and returned it 77 yards for a score.

When you look at the statistics of the Tampa Bay game, it's a wonder we found a way to win. We were outgained by nearly 140 yards and outrushed an incredible 217–64. To me it was a tribute to the character of our team.

The win over Tampa Bay seemed to act as a springboard for us as we went on to win four more in a row, including a 28–10 win in our late October rematch with New England, the team we beat in Super Bowl XXXI nine months earlier. We had our winning streak snapped in one of the biggest NFL upsets in anybody's recent memory: our 41–38 loss to the Indianapolis Colts, who had been winless in ten games prior to that.

It was an embarrassing loss, and it was made worse by the fact that the Colts had their way with us on offense, rolling up 467 yards total. Our offense played exceptionally well that day, but the defense might as well have stayed home. Our linemen were terrible, our linebackers awful, and our defensive backs unspeakable. It was just a terrible performance across the board.

That loss gets back to what I said earlier in this chapter: any team in the NFL is capable of beating any other team on a given Sunday. For whatever reason, we didn't come to play against the Colts, the league's only winless team and up to that point a pretty punchless offensive team, and they made us look really bad.

We tried that week to figure out what went wrong with our defense, but there was really nothing anybody could say. We were terrible, and we knew it. But we also knew what we were capable of, and we knew it was time, as we headed into the final third of the season, to start doing it.

We did just that, and in the process, we broke a couple of Green Bay Packers losing streaks.

## Finishing Strong

When one team consistently beats another, it is often said that the winning team "has their number." That's the way it was with the Dallas Cowboys and the Green Bay Packers in the 1990s. The Cowboys, who had won three Super Bowl championships in the decade, had beaten the Packers eight straight times. Green Bay hadn't beaten the 'Boys since 1989.

That was about to change.

After a first half that ended in a 10–10 tie, we played vintage Green Bay Packers football to take a 45–17 win at Lambeau Field. Dorsey Levens finished with a team record 190 yards rushing, including 145 in the second half as we dominated the Cowboys in every way. Our defense that day was as great against the Cowboys as it had been bad against the Colts. We held Dallas to 213 total yards, including 93 rushing.

Finally it was over. We had ended the Cowboys' mastery over the Packers. Now it was time to end another losing streak: Green Bay's against the Minnesota Vikings at the Metrodome in Minneapolis.

Like the game against the Cowboys, we pulled away in the second half to win going away. Our 27–11 win over the Vikings gave us a 10–3 record and some momentum heading into the final three weeks of the season. We finished with three straight wins—over the Buccaneers in Tampa Bay, the Panthers in Carolina, and the Buffalo Bills in Green Bay. Like we had in 1996, we were heading into the 1997 play-offs with a five-game winning streak. Also like 1996, we had a 13–3 regular season record.

By the end of the season, our offense was clicking, our defense was shutting people down, and we were winning. At that point, it looked like we were ready to accomplish our goal of winning our second straight Super Bowl championship.

## A Tougher Road

The road to Super Bowl XXXII didn't go through Green Bay after the 1997 regular season ended. We had the same record we'd had the previous season, but the San Francisco 49ers, who also finished 13–3, were assured of the home field all the way through the play-offs based on tiebreakers.

We opened the play-offs against the Buccaneers. It wasn't a work of art, but we beat the Bucs 21–7 at Lambeau Field in the divisional play-off game to set up our NFC championship meeting with the 49ers. We had several penalties and dropped passes, sacks on Brett Favre, and 3 turnovers. Dorsey Levens was our big gun on offense, with a team record 112 yards rushing. Our defense was again outstanding, holding Tampa Bay to 264 total yards and one touchdown while harassing Dilfer into a terrible day passing and holding the Tampa Bay running game to 90 yards.

The NFC championship game was played in a wet, windy 3-Com Park in San Francisco. The field was muddy and sloppy—in other words, right up our alley. It was just the kind of weather we'd grown used to in Green Bay, only warmer.

We'd prepared well for the 49ers that week. We found out that we needed to get on their receivers right off the line of scrimmage and stay close to them. We needed to play aggressive pass defense. That strategy paid off big for me and my team.

We led 3–0 in the second quarter, and the 49ers were driving. Then, on a third-and-8 from our 28, I made a play that turned the game in our favor. LeRoy Butler blitzed on the play and was pressuring Steve Young. Brent Jones, San Francisco's tight end, ran an inside route on me and I cut in front of him. I knew the ball would be coming quickly because of the blitz, and it did. I caught the ball and started to my left, then picked up a block by Seth Joyner and headed downfield 58 yards to the San Francisco 28-yard line. After a 1-yard run by Dorsey Levens, Brett Favre threw to Antonio Freeman, who outran the San Francisco secondary for a 27-yard touchdown reception and a 10–0 Green Bay lead.

After the teams exchanged field goals late in the second quarter, we led 13–3 going into the locker room. We extended our lead to 23–3 in the fourth quarter with a field goal by Ryan Longwell and a 5-yard Dorsey Levens touchdown run. At that point, the game was over. Only Chuck Levy's 95-yard kickoff return for a touchdown on our final kickoff made the score respectable.

As the clock wound down and final gun sounded, it hit me and my teammates: we were going back to the Super Bowl.

## Back to the Big Game

When the Green Bay Packers won the NFC championship game in San Francisco, a lot of people thought it was just a formality for us to fly to San Diego and dispose of the AFC champion Denver Broncos in Super Bowl XXXII at Qualcomm Stadium.

We didn't take the Denver Broncos lightly, though. We knew they were a team that had peaked at just the right time. Terrell Davis was a big threat to run the ball, and with John Elway at quarterback, they were also a dangerous passing team. We knew that we had to limit our mistakes—offensively and defensively—because Elway had a way of taking you apart when you messed up. (Believe me, I saw that plenty when I was with the Seahawks, who play in the same division of the AFC as the Broncos.)

The Broncos had had trouble stopping the run that season, but they had improved as the year went on. Neil Smith, who had signed as a free agent from Kansas City at the start of the season, and Alfred Williams were an imposing pair of defensive ends who could make life rough for Brett Favre. And they had Steve Atwater and Tyrone Braxton patrolling their defensive backfield.

We knew we weren't in for a cakewalk, but there was no doubt in our minds that we could beat them. We knew we had to play well and limit our mistakes.

Like Super Bowl XXXI and all the Super Bowls before it, the Big Game in San Diego was built up with the typical media hype. Again, I enjoyed Super Bowl week and talking to all the reporters. I enjoyed being with my team-mates that week as we prepared for the game. I especially enjoyed the national anthem and the rest of the pregame ceremonies.

The pregame ceremonies at Super Bowl XXXII were amazing. The fans were treated to a beautiful rendition of the national anthem by Jewel, who sang as they brought out a huge flag that was so big that they had to have guys standing under it to keep it from touching the ground. That was fol-lowed by a flyover by the Blue Angels.

That gave me goose bumps. But what I saw next was something I'll never forget. I looked up after the Blue Angels had passed, and I saw it: a Stealth Bomber. I hadn't heard it fly over, and I wouldn't have known it was there had I not looked up. It came in from my left, and as I spotted it, I pointed it out to my teammates. "Look at that!" I said, and we all watched in amazement.

For just a few minutes, I was like a fan, just standing there soaking all this in. It was an impressive display. But it didn't stop there, as Super Bowl XXXII turned out to be, in the minds of most people, the greatest ever played.

## A Game to Remember

For years, football fans had grown resigned to what had become Super Bowl tradition: the NFC team blows the AFC representative off the field. Thirteen straight Super Bowls had gone to the NFC team, and most of them weren't close. Most people expected the thirty-second Super Bowl to be much the same, with the Packers taking control early and coasting home with the win.

Early in the game, it looked like that would be the case. We took the ball at our own 24-yard line on our first possession and drove down the field relatively easily, scoring in eight plays on Brett Favre's 22-yard touchdown pass to Antonio Freeman to make it 7–0 just over four minutes into the game. That, it turns out, would be our only lead of the game.

Vaughn Hebron got the Broncos started with a 32-yard kickoff return to the Denver 42. From there, Elway led them on a 10-play drive for Terrell Davis's 1-yard touchdown run. After Tyrone Braxton intercepted a Brett Favre pass at the Packer 45-yard line, the Broncos drove for a 1-yard touchdown run by Elway. A 51-yard field goal by Jason Elam following a fumble made it 17–7.

Two possessions later, the Packers drove a club postseason record 95 yards in 17 plays to score on Brett Favre's 6-yard touchdown pass to tight end Mark Chmura with twelve seconds left in the half to make it 17–14 at halftime. Ryan Longwell tied the game for us with a field goal after Terrell Davis fumbled on the first play from scrimmage in the second half.

Later in the third quarter, Elway took the Broncos on a 92-yard drive for another 1-yard touchdown run by Terrell Davis. Late in the drive, Elway made one of the key plays in the game—and one of the greatest plays in Super Bowl history. The Broncos had driven to the Green Bay 12-yard line, where they faced third down with 6 yards to go. Elway dropped back to pass on the play but found nobody open. He took off and ran down the middle of the field, then cut right, where he met LeRoy Butler near the first-down marker. As LeRoy lowered his shoulder to hit Elway, the Denver quarterback leaped into the air and took the blow in such a way that it spun him around in midair, where he took another hit by Mike Prior. When the play was over, the Broncos had the ball at the 4-yard line with a first-and-goal. Denver scored two plays later to make it 24–17.

The Broncos had a chance to take a 1-touchdown lead on the ensuing kickoff, which we fumbled at our own 22-yard line. Elway threw to the end zone, but I made the interception 2 yards deep and returned it to our 15. Brett Favre then led us on a quick four-play scoring drive of 85 yards, capping it off with a 13-yard scoring pass to Antonio Freeman.

Denver scored the winning touchdown two possessions later, driving 49 yards in five plays, including Davis's 1-yard touchdown run with 1:45 left in the game. That final touchdown run was one of the strangest plays in Super Bowl history for one reason: we let Davis score. Realizing that we were running out of time to tie the score and that the Broncos were going to score, Coach Holmgren instructed us to concede the touchdown so that we'd have time to come back to tie the score.

We took over the ball at our own 30 on the ensuing kickoff, then drove quickly to the Denver 35. But a short Dorsey Levens run followed by 3 straight incompletions from Brett Favre ended our hopes of repeating as Super Bowl champions.

## Giving the Broncos Their Due

There has been a lot of talk about how the Broncos' Super Bowl win was a fluke. It was anything but a fluke. There was a very simple reason why the Broncos won: they played better than we did. They were a great team by the time they reached the Super Bowl, and they played a superb game to beat us. They kept their mistakes to a minimum, and they got a great game from Terrell Davis, who finished with 179 yards rushing. He had plenty of help, too, as the Broncos' offensive line, the league's lightest, wore down our front four.

Super Bowl XXXII was also a continuation of the legend of John Elway. John didn't have a great game statistically, but he did what it took to beat us. I still have to tip my hat to the man when I think about the run for a first down late in the third quarter. It was an example of someone sacrificing his own body for the good of his team. I can't help but respect him for that.

While I was disappointed for us that we lost in Super Bowl XXXII, I was happy for John Elway, Steve Atwater, and the rest of those guys. They deserved what they got that day, and they had my congratulations.

I also felt an incredible amount of gratitude toward God, who blessed us throughout a great ride to two Super Bowls.

## Give Him the Glory

That night, though we were disappointed and hurt that we'd lost in Super Bowl XXXII, we still praised God for all that he'd done for us. We praised him because he was still on his throne, because he still loved us, and because he was still God. We praised him because he was still using us to glorify himself.

God continues to be God regardless of what happens in our lives. When we succeed in what we set out to do, we praise him and give him glory. When we fall short, what do we do? We still praise him and give him the glory.

My main objective in life—to lift up Jesus Christ before men—doesn't change with my circumstances. I praised God when we won my first Super Bowl, and I continued to praise him when we lost the following year. I'd much rather have won than lost that day. That was my objective from day one of the 1997 training camp. We fell short of that goal, but that doesn't change my life's objectives.

I didn't mope around the house after we lost and I didn't blame myself, my teammates, or the coaches. Instead, I looked to Jesus Christ, who I know wants to make me a better person, a more complete man of God, whether I win or lose. I believe that God uses something as insignificant—in the eternal context—as losing a football game to make me more like Jesus Christ. The Bible tells me, "being confident of this, that he who began a good work in you will carry it on to completion until the day of Christ Jesus" (Philippians 1:6).

Nobody in the NFL enjoys losing. I have always done everything I could to win. But I can't win every game. Even the best teams in the world lose once in a while. But in terms of God's eternal plan, that's okay. He'll use that and other things that people might consider failure to make me a better person. And with his help, I can endure disappointment.

With him, I can endure anything.

## CHAPTER THIRTEEN

## A LIFE OF ENDURANCE

# DRAWING CLOSE TO GOD

t's amazing to me when I think about the way God has blessed me—in my family life, in my career, with friends. It's impossible for me to fully put into words the gratitude I feel toward my God for blessing me and using me the way he has.

I know that won't end when I'm done playing football, either. I know God has more great things in store for me, simply because I'm committed to living for him, because I have chosen to endure the road he's sent me to follow. I know that whatever my next phase in life is, God will be there, providing me opportunities to do what I like doing best: telling people about Jesus Christ.

These are the blessings of enduring the tests and trials that are sure to come with the Christian life. I've had a great life, serving God and loving my family and friends. But I, like anybody else who calls Jesus "Lord," have endured some tough tests and trials. That's the way it is with the Christian life. That's the way God designed it.

When you come to Christ in faith, you don't just ask for forgiveness and a ticket to heaven, and that's the end of it. You give him yourself to do with as he pleases. You come to him agreeing that you are a sinner and that there is nothing you can do about that condition on your own. You yield to him, allowing him to change you into the person he wants you to be. That's when the changes start. Changes in the way you think and in the way you live.

That's where the conflicts start. Inner conflicts and conflicts with the world around you.

I would be remiss not to tell you that living the Christian life isn't easy.

Nowhere in the Bible does it say that it will be. In fact, the Bible promises us all kinds of trials and tests when we decide to follow Jesus Christ. It promises that this sinful old world will persecute us for following Jesus. Some may lose friends on account of him, and others may find themselves ostracized from their families. Others may be mocked and avoided, and some may even have to give up their lives.

In America, we have it pretty easy right now. It's safe to say that if you profess Christ in front of somebody, the worst that will happen is that you'll be ridiculed or avoided. You probably won't undergo any real physical persecution.

That doesn't mean, though, that there won't be trials. The Bible says that those who attempt to live holy lives will undergo tests in this world. They'll be tested because the enemy—the devil—doesn't like people living for God. He doesn't like it when your words and actions bring glory to the Father. He doesn't like it when you commit all that you do and say to Jesus Christ.

And if he doesn't like that, he violently hates it when you tell others about Jesus Christ, and he'll try everything within his power to keep you from doing just that.

Does that sound easy to you? Believe me, it's not! There's an old saying about doing something that is difficult that goes like this: "If it were easy, anybody could do it." The truth of the matter is that I can't live a victorious Christian life. Neither can you. Nobody can. We are, in fact, helpless when it comes to serving God. We are bound to failure.

Unless…

## Strength to Endure

By now, you're probably thinking, *Eugene Robinson is telling me that I need Jesus Christ, that I should have a personal relationship with him. I'll buy that, but I don't like the sound of going through the trials that come just because I'm a Christian. Now he's saying it's not possible for me to succeed in the Christian life! What's up with that?*

It's true that God promises that as Christians we'll face tough times in this world and that some of them won't be fun. It's even true that Jesus said, "Apart from me you can do nothing" (John 15:5). I can tell you from personal experience that these things are true. It's tough to live a Christian life. In fact, it's impossible...unless you're walking in the power of Christ that is provided us through the ministry of the Holy Spirit.

Jesus promised us in Matthew 28:20 that he would stand by us always, including when we face tough times. It still won't be easy, but it will be something you can do because God is right there, encouraging you and giving you strength.

## Draw Near to Him

Over the years I've known a lot of people who have been beaten down by the enemy. The devil has had a field day with some brothers in Christ I've known, guys who truly want to live for the Lord. I've talked with these guys, and I hear stuff like this:

> "Gene, I don't know what to do. I want to serve God and I want to
> live right before him, but it ain't happening. It just seems like I can't
> win. What should I do?"

In a situation like that, I ask some basic questions: "Are you reading your Bible? Are you praying? Are you in fellowship with other brothers and sisters in Christ?"

More often than not, when somebody is struggling like that—losing the battle, really—they're not doing the things they need to do in order to draw near to God.

If you want to endure the tests this world is going to throw at you, you've got to tap into the power source that God has made available to you. You've got to get closer to him. You've got to do what James 4:8 says: "Draw near to God and he will draw near to you." And how do you draw near to God? The same way you draw close to another human: by communicating with him.

If you want to endure in the Christian life, you've got to feed what the apostle Paul called the "inner man." Do you remember when I talked about Dave Brown challenging me, telling me that I couldn't nourish my soul with food? He was right. You can't feed your soul or your spirit with food. That inner part of you, the part where Christ dwells when you become a Christian, has to be fed through the Word, prayer, and fellowship with other believers.

## Living in the Word

Read your Bible! Read it, memorize it, think about it! Read it and re-read it!

The Word of God is life, spiritual life, and you've got to tap into that spiritual life if you're going to endure. You've got to know the Word and apply it to your own life. You've got to be able to draw on your knowledge of the Word when you are faced with a test or trial.

I want to encourage you to make reading and memorizing Scripture a priority in your life. Read your Bible every day. I recommend that you get involved in a Bible study or that you purchase a study guide to use when you read your Bible.

When you read your Bible, take the time to ask yourself some key questions: What does this mean? and What does this mean *to me?* You need to know what the Word says and how you can apply it to your own life, in your own present situation. When you do that, the Word of God will come alive to you like it never has before.

## You've Got to Pray

Reading your Bible is great, and memorizing it is excellent. But you also need to accompany your study of the Word with prayer. Simply put, you've got to talk to God.

I want you to know that God wants to hear from you. He created people in the first place so that he could have fellowship with a being that could respond to his love. That fellowship was broken when sin entered the picture, but it was restored when Jesus Christ came to earth, died on the cross, and rose from the dead—all so God could pay for the terrible consequences of our sin.

When you pray, come to God with thanksgiving and praise. Tell him how much you appreciate all he's done for you. Give him praise just because he's God. Then come to him with your requests. Talk to him about your needs, the needs of your friends and family; talk to him about someone you know who needs salvation.

When you pray for these things, believe God will answer your prayers. When the answers don't come right away, keep praying. Don't give up. God always answers your prayers, but sometimes he waits a while before he does it. Keep praying and believing!

## Spending Time in Fellowship

You can study your Bible and pray on your own, but you should also make time to do those things in the company of other believers. God didn't create us to be alone, but sometimes young Christians behave as though he did. They don't spend time with other believers, and then wonder why they struggle so much.

You need the encouragement that being in fellowship with other Christians brings. It's amazing to me how being around other believers strengthens and encourages me. I've needed that at times, too. I'm sure you do also.

If you're not in fellowship at a local church, find one, and start going. Plug yourself in by getting involved in some of the church's events outside of Sunday morning services. Go to Sunday school, Bible studies, fellowship groups…whatever your church offers, take advantage of it!

Find people with whom you can talk about the things of God, and if you're a young believer, find someone who can mentor or disciple you. You'll find that the rewards for doing this are great.

## Endurance: Rejoicing in Trials

When you do the things that help you endure the trials that come in the Christian life, you will be able to do as the apostle James wrote in James 1:2:

"Consider it pure joy, my brothers, whenever you face trials of many kinds, because you know that the testing of your faith develops perseverance."

That's right! We can actually rejoice in the fact that there are trials in our lives, knowing that they only make us stronger. We can look at the trials and tests and actually welcome them as tools to make us more mature and complete in Jesus Christ.

Choosing to live for Jesus Christ and endure tests and trials for him is one of the toughest things you can do. But it's the best decision you'll ever make!

And once you've made that decision, hang in there. Be strong. Endure!

And when you do, you will be a recipient of the promise of God as recorded in 1 Corinthians 1:8: "He will keep you strong to the end, so that you will be blameless on the day of our Lord Jesus Christ."

What a day that will be!

# MOVING ON—AGAIN

When Super Bowl XXXII ended, so did my employment with the Green Bay Packers. I played two years in Titletown before it was time to move on.

The Packers made it clear that they were going a different direction at free safety, and that Darren Sharper, a player I helped groom to take over my position while I was with the Packers, would be pushed into the role of starter. Packers fans can rest assured knowing that they have a talented player who will excel for many years to come at the free-safety position.

I, on the other hand, wanted to play, and it became apparent that I would need to go somewhere else in order to continue starting. I wasn't ready to be a backup, and signing with the Atlanta Falcons will give me the opportunity to play.

I left the Packers with the greatest appreciation for a great two-year ride. We won a lot of football games, played in two Super Bowls, and had a wonderful time. And those of us on the Packers who know the Lord Jesus Christ also had the time of our lives, glorifying God as we played Packers football.

It became apparent after the 1997 season that God was moving me and my family to Atlanta. My wife and I believe in the power of prayer and in a God who works on our behalf. At first, Gia was against us going to Atlanta; in fact, she prayed against it. But we continued to pray about it and seek God's guidance, and soon her heart—a heart that cared only about serving God and taking care of her family—changed. We agreed that this was the right move for us.

My daughter and my son both agreed to the move, too. Brittany looks forward to the move with excitement, knowing that she'll have a whole new world of friends and things to do in a new setting. Brandon just wants his dad to get his fiftieth interception before he retires. (I currently have forty-nine, which leads all active players.)

My family was behind our move, the money was right, and I would have a chance to close out my career as a full-time player. It was all set. I signed with Atlanta.

Right now, I'm planning to play one more year. The Falcons want me to play two, but I don't know. I know that God will guide me and Gia as we decide what to do at the end of the 1998 season.

I also know that God will guide me when I finally retire from the NFL. I know he has a plan for me, and I look forward to seeing that plan unfold when I'm done with football. Whatever that plan turns out to be, I know God will continue to allow me to serve him in whatever I'm doing.

That's something I can count on!

# A EUGENE ROBINSON PROFILE

## Personal:

Resides in Woodinville, Washington, with wife, Gia, and two children: daughter Brittany (born August 12, 1987) and son Brandon (born January 16, 1990).

Born May 28, 1963 in Hartford, Connecticut, to parents Samuel and Marcella Robinson. Full name is Eugene Keefe Robinson. Youngest of four children. Sisters Deborah and Renee, and brother Samuel.

Boyhood football hero was Minnesota Vikings running back Chuck Foreman.

Hobbies include playing the saxophone and computer programming. Eugene is also a jazz music enthusiast and owns a large collection of jazz compact disks.

## High School:

Attended Weaver High School in Hartford, where he made the National Honor Roll and played football and wrestled. Took top three finishes in state wrestling tournament during sophomore and junior years.

English teacher Jannie Phillips was named NFL Teacher of the Month for December, 1991.

## College:

Attended Colgate University in Hamilton, New York. Earned B.S. degree in Computer Science. Not recruited as football player out of high school, but walked on and played football all four years for the Red Raiders (1981–84).

Played junior varsity football during freshman season. Two-year starter and three-year letterman for Colgate varsity. Finished college career with 120 tackles and 4 interceptions, including 52 tackles and 2 interceptions as a senior.

## Pro:

- Undrafted in 1985 National Football League draft but signed as free agent with Seattle Seahawks and earned spot on team as a rookie as reserve safety and special teams player. Played eleven seasons with Seattle.
- Leads active players with 49 career interceptions.
- Tied for National Football League lead in interceptions (with Buffalo's Nate Odomes) with 9 in 1993 season.
- Named to the Pro Bowl following 1992 and 1993 seasons.
- Forty-two interceptions with Seahawks ranks him second all-time on the team. Led Seattle in interceptions in six of his last seven seasons there.
- Seattle's all-time leading tackler with 983. Tied for club record with four 100-tackle seasons. Led Seahawks in tackles four times.
- Voted defensive captain by Seahawk teammates four straight seasons (1992–95).
- Named Seattle's NFL Man of the Year four times (1991–93, 1995).
- Traded by Seahawks to the Green Bay Packers for defensive end Matt LaBounty prior to the 1996 season. Member of Super Bowl XXXI champion Packers.
- Signed with Atlanta Falcons as unrestricted free agent prior to 1998 season.

## PRO STATISTICS REGULAR SEASON

| YEAR | TEAM | G/S | UT | TT | INT | YDS | FF | FR | TDF | S |
|------|------|-----|-----|-----|-----|-----|-----|-----|-----|-----|
| 1985 | Sea. | 16/0 | 18 | 28 | 2 | 47 | 0 | 0 | 0 | 0 |
| 1986 | Sea. | 16/16 | 81 | 99 | 3 | 39 | 0 | 3 | 0 | 0 |

| 1987 | Sea. | 12/12 | 50 | 69 | 3 | 75 | 0 | 1 | 1 | 0 |
|------|------|-------|----|----|---|----|----|----|----|----|
| 1988 | Sea. | 16/16 | 86 | 115 | 1 | 0 | 1 | 0 | 0 | 1 |
| 1989 | Sea. | 16/14 | 76 | 107 | 5 | 24 | 2 | 1 | 0 | 0 |
| 1990 | Sea. | 16/16 | 63 | 82 | 3 | 89 | 1 | 4 | 1 | 0 |
| 1991 | Sea. | 16/16 | 69 | 93 | 5 | 56 | 1 | 1 | 0 | 1 |
| 1992 | Sea. | 16/16 | 64 | 94 | 7 | 126 | 2 | 1 | 0 | 0 |
| 1993 | Sea. | 16/16 | 84 | 111 | 9 | 80 | 3 | 2 | 0 | 2 |
| 1994 | Sea. | 16/14 | 65 | 80 | 3 | 18 | 0 | 3 | 0 | 1 |
| 1995 | Sea. | 16/16 | 79 | 105 | 1 | 32 | 0 | 0 | 0 | 0 |
| 1996 | G.B. | 16/16 | 55 | 81 | 6 | 107 | 0 | 0 | 0 | 0 |
| 1997 | G.B. | 16/16 | 75 | 112 | 1 | 26 | 1 | 1 | 0 | 2.5 |

13 Season Totals

| | | 204/184 | 865 | 1,176 | 49 | 719 | 11 | 17 | 2 | 7.5 |
|--|--|---------|-----|-------|----|----|----|----|----|-----|

## In Select Company

Eugene Robinson leads the active players in career interceptions. Here is how he ranks among active players in interceptions and in return yards:

**Interceptions**

| Player | No. |
|--------|-----|
| Eugene Robinson | 49 |
| Darrell Green | 44 |
| Rod Woodson | 41 |
| Albert Lewis | 40 |
| Eric Allen | 39 |
| Eugene Daniel | 38 |
| Kevin Ross | 38 |
| Aeneas Williams | 38 |
| Lionel Washington | 37 |
| 2 tied with | 36 |

**Interception Return Yards**

| Player | Yards |
|--------|-------|
| Deion Sanders | 941 |
| Rod Woodson | 860 |
| Eugene Robinson | 719 |
| Kevin Ross | 654 |
| Terry McDaniel | 624 |
| Tim McDonald | 600 |
| Eric Allen | 570 |
| Darryl Williams | 557 |
| Tyrone Braxton | 545 |
| 2 tied with | 531 |

Paul Krause, who played sixteen years in the National Football League, is the league's top all-time intercepter with 81. Here is how Eugene Robinson ranks with the all-time leaders:

| Player (years) | No. | Player (years) | No. |
|---|---|---|---|
| Paul Krause (16) | 81 | Jake Scott (9) | 49 |
| Emlen Tunnell (14) | 79 | **Eugene Robinson (13)** | **49** |
| Dick Lane (68) | 68 | Richie Pettibon (15) | 48 |
| Ken Riley (15) | 65 | Willie Wood (12) | 48 |
| Ronnie Lott (14) | 63 | Dave Grayson (10) | 48 |
| Dave Brown (15) | 62 | Herb Adderly (12) | 48 |
| Dick LeBeau (13) | 62 | Dave Waymer (13) | 48 |
| Emmitt Thomas (13) | 58 | | |
| Bobby Boyd (9) | 57 | | |
| Johnny Robinson (12) | 57 | | |
| Mel Blount (14) | 57 | | |
| Everson Walls (13) | 57 | | |
| Lem Barney (11) | 56 | | |
| Pat Fischer (17) | 56 | | |
| Willie Brown (16) | 54 | | |
| Bobbie Dillon (8) | 52 | | |
| Jack Butler (9) | 52 | | |
| Larry Wilson (13) | 52 | | |
| Jim Patton (12) | 52 | | |
| Mel Renfro (14) | 52 | | |
| Bobby Bryant (13) | 51 | | |
| Donnie Shell (14) | 51 | | |
| Yale Larry (13) | 50 | | |
| Don Burroughs (10) | 50 | | |
| John Harris (11) | 50 | | |
| Deron Cherry (11) | 50 | | |
| Ken Houston (14) | 49 | | |

# CHAMPIONSHIP HISTORY

## Super Bowl Results

| NO. | YEAR | SITE | RESULT |
| --- | --- | --- | --- |
| 32 | 1998 | San Diego | Denver 31, Green Bay 24 |
| 31 | 1997 | New Orleans | Green Bay 35, New England 21 |
| 30 | 1996 | Tempe | Dallas 27, Pittsburgh 17 |
| 29 | 1995 | Miami | San Francisco 49, San Diego 26 |
| 28 | 1994 | Atlanta | Dallas 30, Buffalo 13 |
| 27 | 1993 | Pasadena | Dallas 52, Buffalo 17 |
| 26 | 1992 | Minneapolis | Washington 37, Buffalo 24 |
| 25 | 1991 | Tampa | New York Giants 20, Buffalo 19 |
| 24 | 1990 | New Orleans | San Francisco 55, Denver 10 |
| 23 | 1989 | Miama | San Francisco 20, Cincinnati 16 |
| 22 | 1988 | San Diego | Washington 42, Denver 10 |
| 21 | 1987 | Pasadena | New York Giants 39, Denver 20 |
| 20 | 1986 | New Orleans | Chicago 46, New England 10 |
| 19 | 1985 | Stanford | San Francisco 38, Miami 16 |
| 18 | 1984 | Tampa | L. A. Raiders 38, Washington 9 |
| 17 | 1983 | Pasadena | Washington 27, Miami 17 |
| 16 | 1982 | Pontiac | San Francisco 16, Cincinnati 21 |
| 15 | 1981 | New Orleans | Oakland 27, Philadelphia 10 |
| 14 | 1980 | Pasadena | Pittsburgh 31, L. A. Rams 19 |
| 13 | 1979 | Miami | Pittsburgh 35, Dallas 31 |
| 12 | 1978 | New Orleans | Dallas 27, Denver 10 |
| 11 | 1977 | Pasadena | Oakland 32, Minnesota 14 |
| 10 | 1976 | Miami | Pittsburgh 21, Dallas 17 |

| 9 | 1975 | New Orleans | Pittsburgh 16, Minnesota 6 |
| 8 | 1974 | Houston | Miami 24, Minnesota 7 |
| 7 | 1973 | Los Angeles | Miami 14, Washington 7 |
| 6 | 1972 | New Orleans | Dallas 24, Miami 3 |
| 5 | 1971 | Miami | Baltimore 16, Dallas 13 |
| 4 | 1970 | New Orleans | Kansas City 23, Minnesota 7 |
| 3 | 1969 | Miami | New York Jets 16, Baltimore 7 |
| 2 | 1968 | Miami | Green Bay 33, Oakland 14 |
| 1 | 1967 | Los Angeles | Green Bay 35, Kansas City 10 |

## Green Bay Packers All-Time Play-off Results

| DATE | GAME | RESULT |
| --- | --- | --- |
| 1–25–98 | Super Bowl XXXII | Denver 31, Green Bay 24 |
| 1–11–98 | NFC Championship | Green Bay 23, San Francisco 10 |
| 1–4–98 | NFC Divisional | Green Bay 21, Tampa Bay 7 |
| 1–26–97 | Super Bowl XXXI | Green Bay 35, New England 21 |
| 1–12–97 | NFC Championship | Green Bay 30, Carolina 13 |
| 1–4–97 | NFC Divisional | Green Bay 35, San Francisco 14 |
| 1–13–96 | NFC Championship | Dallas 38, Green Bay 27 |
| 1–6–96 | NFC Divisional | Green Bay 27, San Francisco 17 |
| 12–31–95 | NFC Wild Card | Green Bay 27, Atlanta 20 |
| 1–8–95 | NFC Divisional | Dallas 35, Green Bay 9 |
| 1–1–95 | NFC Wild Card | Green Bay 16, Detroit 12 |
| 1–16–94 | NFC Divisional | Dallas 27, Green Bay 17 |
| 1–8–94 | NFC Wild Card | Green Bay 28, Detroit 24 |
| 1–16–83 | NFC Divisional | Dallas 37, Green Bay 26 |
| 1–8–83 | NFC Wild Card | Green Bay 41, St. Louis 16 |
| 12–24–72 | NFC Divisional | Washington 16, Green Bay 3 |
| 1–14–68 | Super Bowl II | Green Bay 33, Oakland 14 |
| 12–31–67 | NFL Championship | Green Bay 21, Dallas 17 |
| 12–23–67 | NFL Divisional | Green Bay 28, L. A. Rams 7 |

| | | |
|---|---|---|
| 1–15–67 | Super Bowl I | Green Bay 35, Kansas City 10 |
| 1–1–67 | NFL Championship | Green Bay 31, Dallas 27 |
| 1–2–66 | NFL Championship | Green Bay 23, Cleveland 12 |
| 12–26–65 | NFL Divisional | Green Bay 13, Baltimore 10 (ot) |
| 12–30–62 | NFL Championship | Green Bay 16, New York 7 |
| 12–31–61 | NFL Championship | Green Bay 37, New York 0 |
| 12–26–60 | NFL Championship | Philadelphia 17, Green Bay 14 |
| 12–17–44 | NFL Championship | Green Bay 14, New York 7 |
| 12–14–41 | NFL Divisional | Chicago 33, Green Bay 14 |
| 12–10–39 | NFL Championship | Green Bay 27, New York 0 |
| 12–11–38 | NFL Championship | New York 23, Green Bay 17 |
| 12–13–36 | NFL Championship | Green Bay 21, Boston 6 |